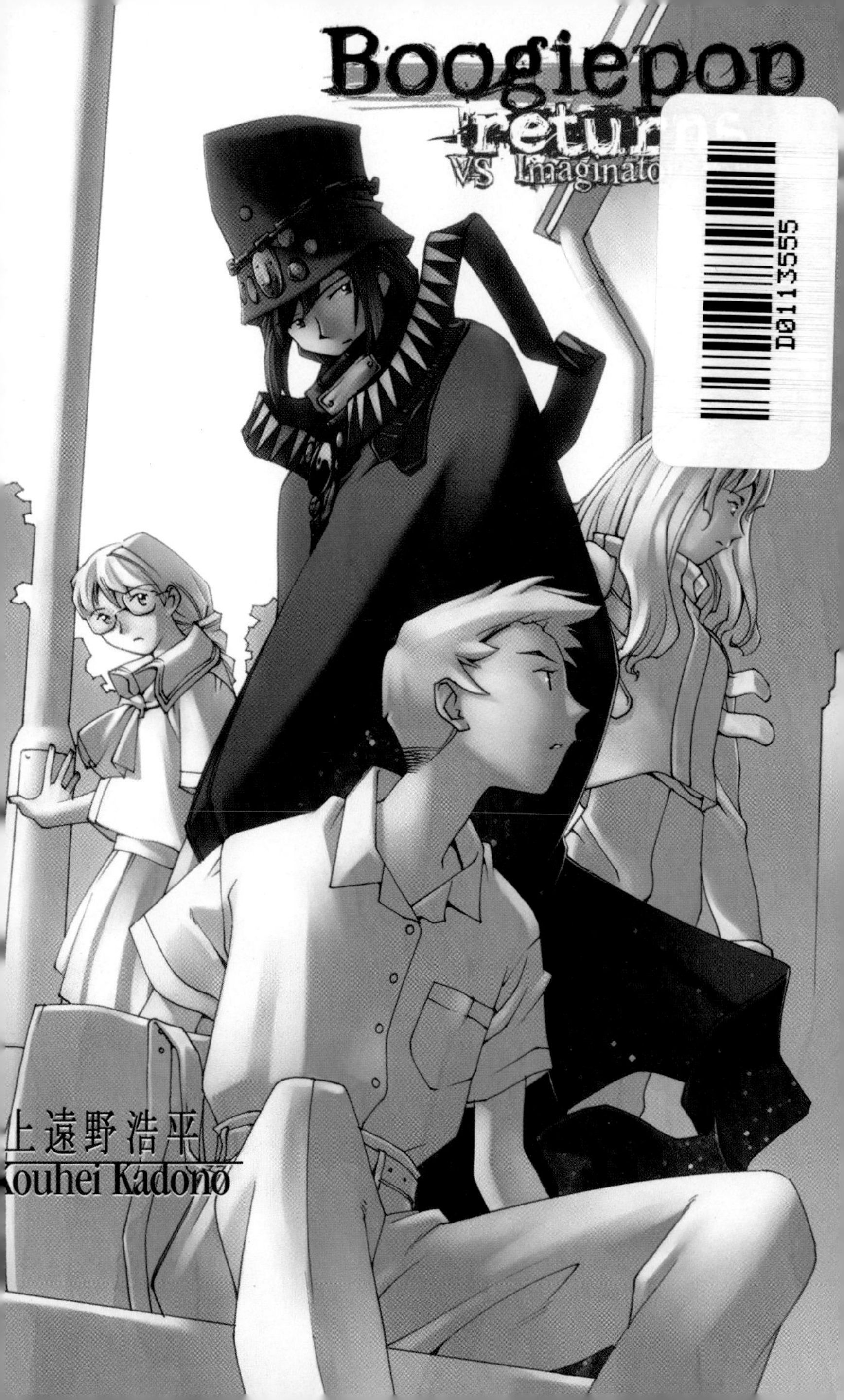
Boogiepop
retur
VS Imaginato
上遠野浩平
Kouhei Kadono

"Is there anything you'd like me to do? Go ahead, ask me anything."

– Taniguchi Masaki

"I have no right to dislike anything."

– Orihata Aya

"If you aren't useful to me…
I'll dispose of you whenever I wish."

– Spooky E

"Why am I crying?"

– Anou Shinjirou

"There's nothing in this world that is ever truly decided."

— Minahoshi Suiko

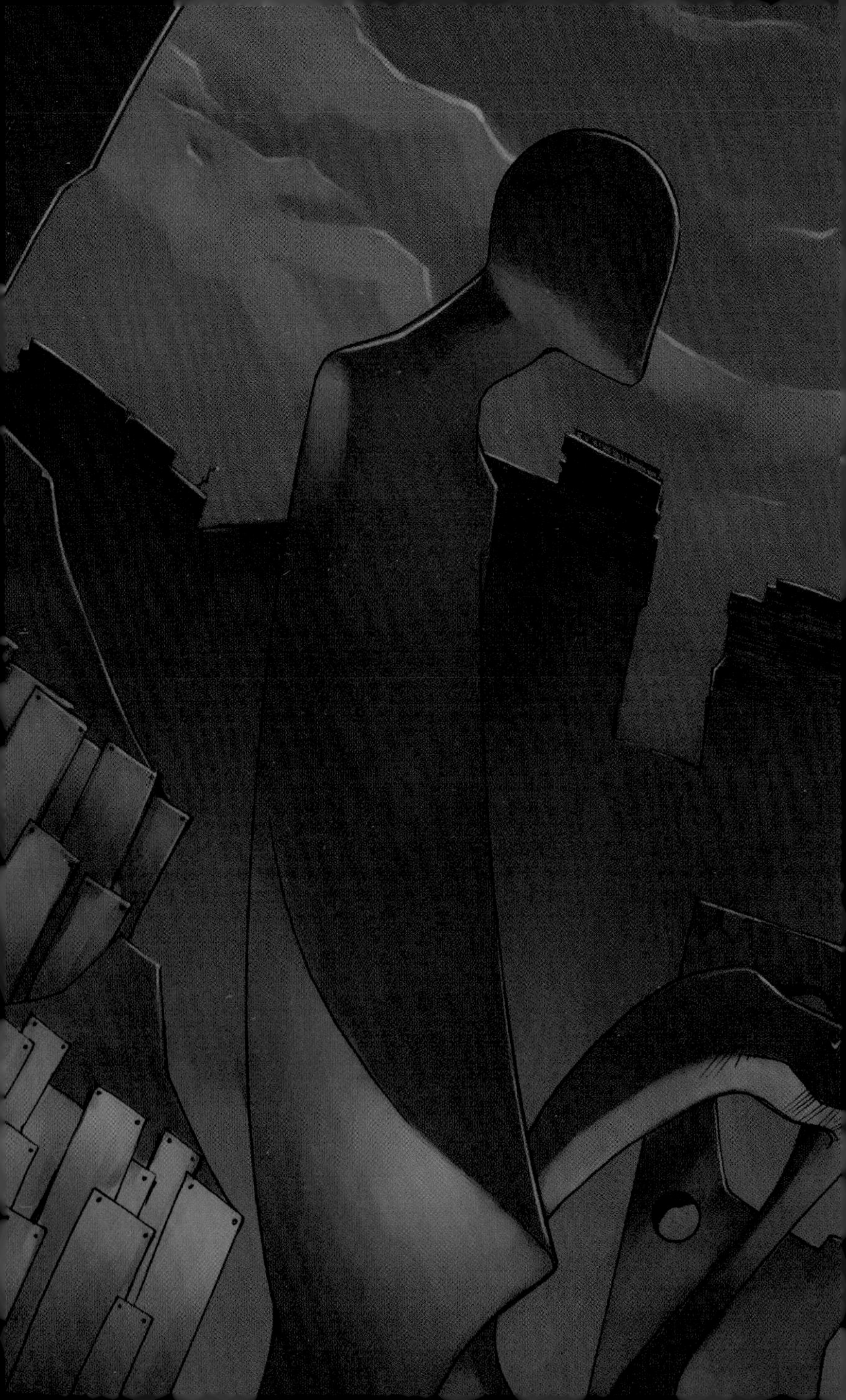

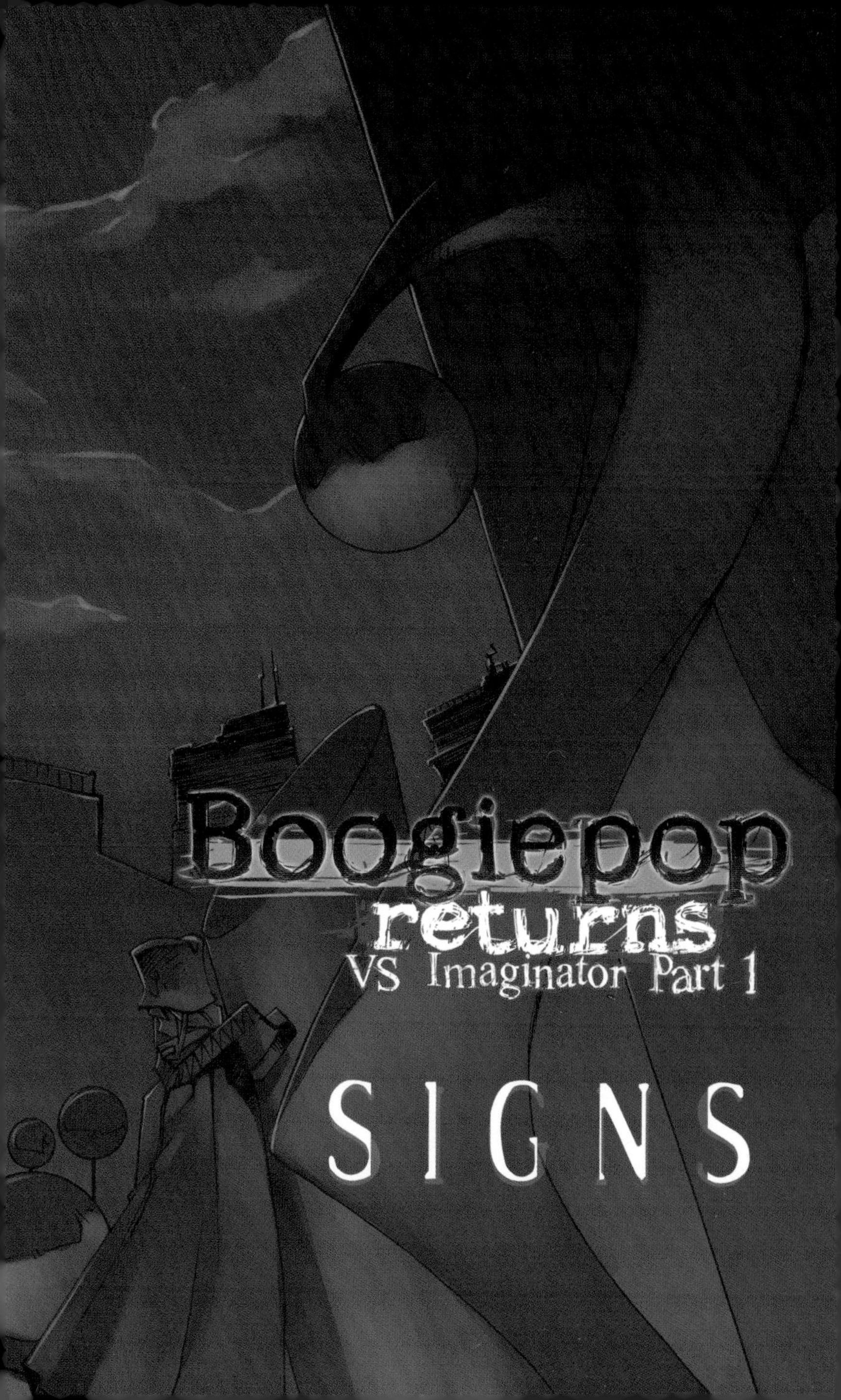
Boogiepop
returns
VS Imaginator Part 1
SIGNS

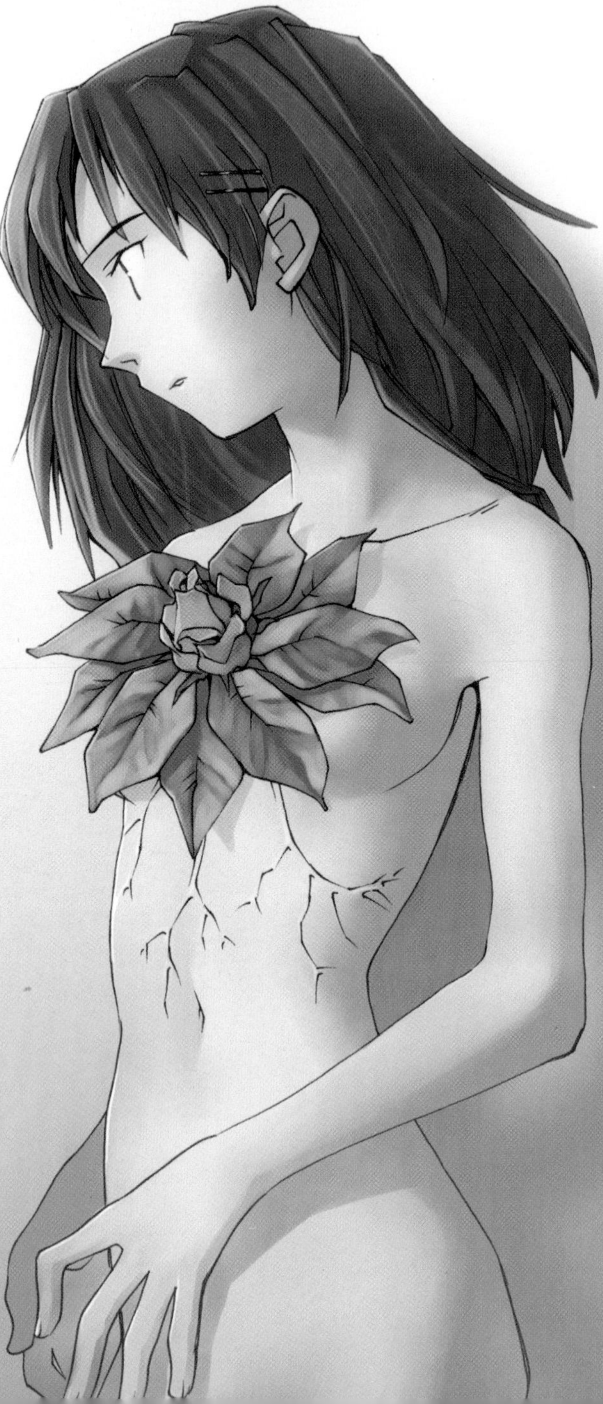

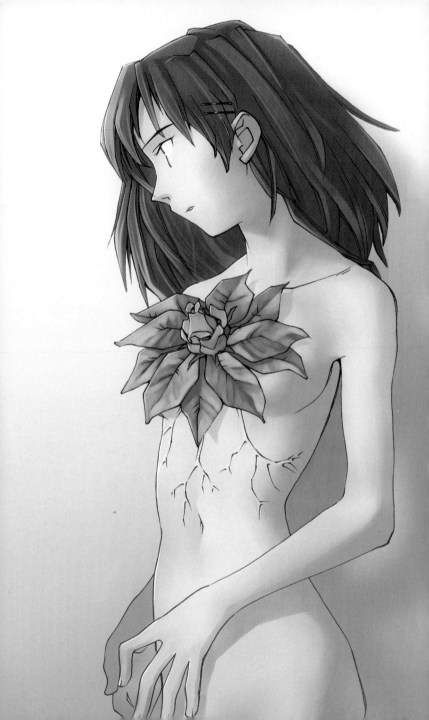

Boogiepop returns
VS Imaginator Part 1

Boogiepop returns
VS Imaginator Part 1

written by
Kouhei Kadono

illustrated by
Kouji Ogata

english translation by
Andrew Cunningham

Seven Seas

LOS ANGELES

BOOGIEPOP RETURNS: VS IMAGINATOR PART 1
© KOUHEI KADONO 1998
First published in 1998 by Media Works Inc., Tokyo, Japan.
English translation rights arranged with Media Works Inc.

STAFF CREDITS

English Translation: Andrew Cunningham
Layout and Graphic Design: Nicky Lim
Assistant Editor: Jason DeAngelis
Editor: Adam Arnold

Publisher: Seven Seas Entertainment

Visit us online at **www.gomanga.com.**

1-933164-20-4

Printed in Canada

First printing: April, 2006

10 9 8 7 6 5 4 3 2 1

table of contents

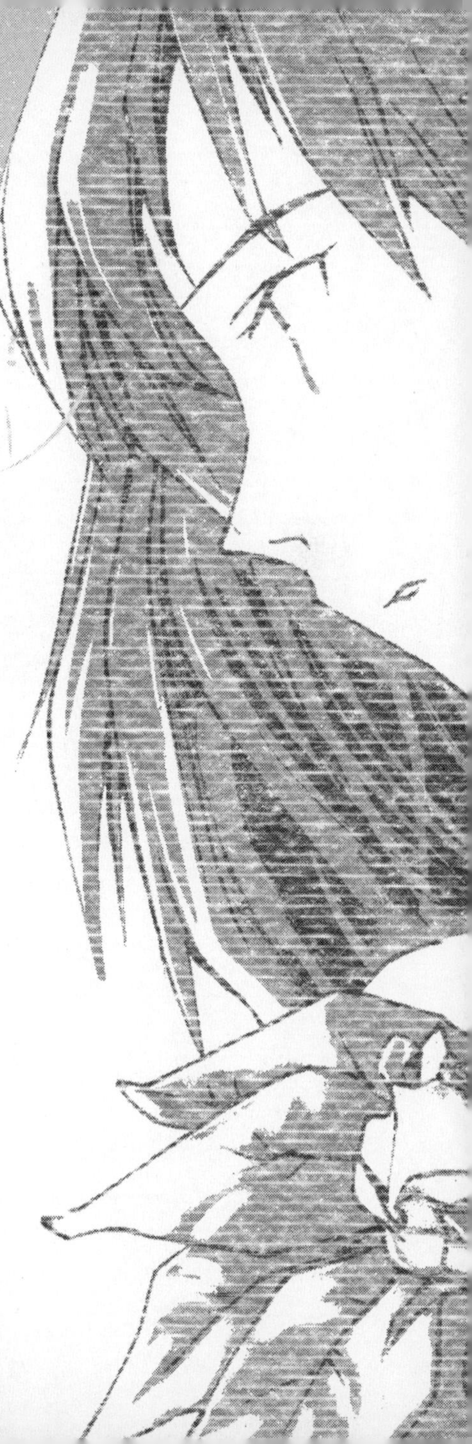

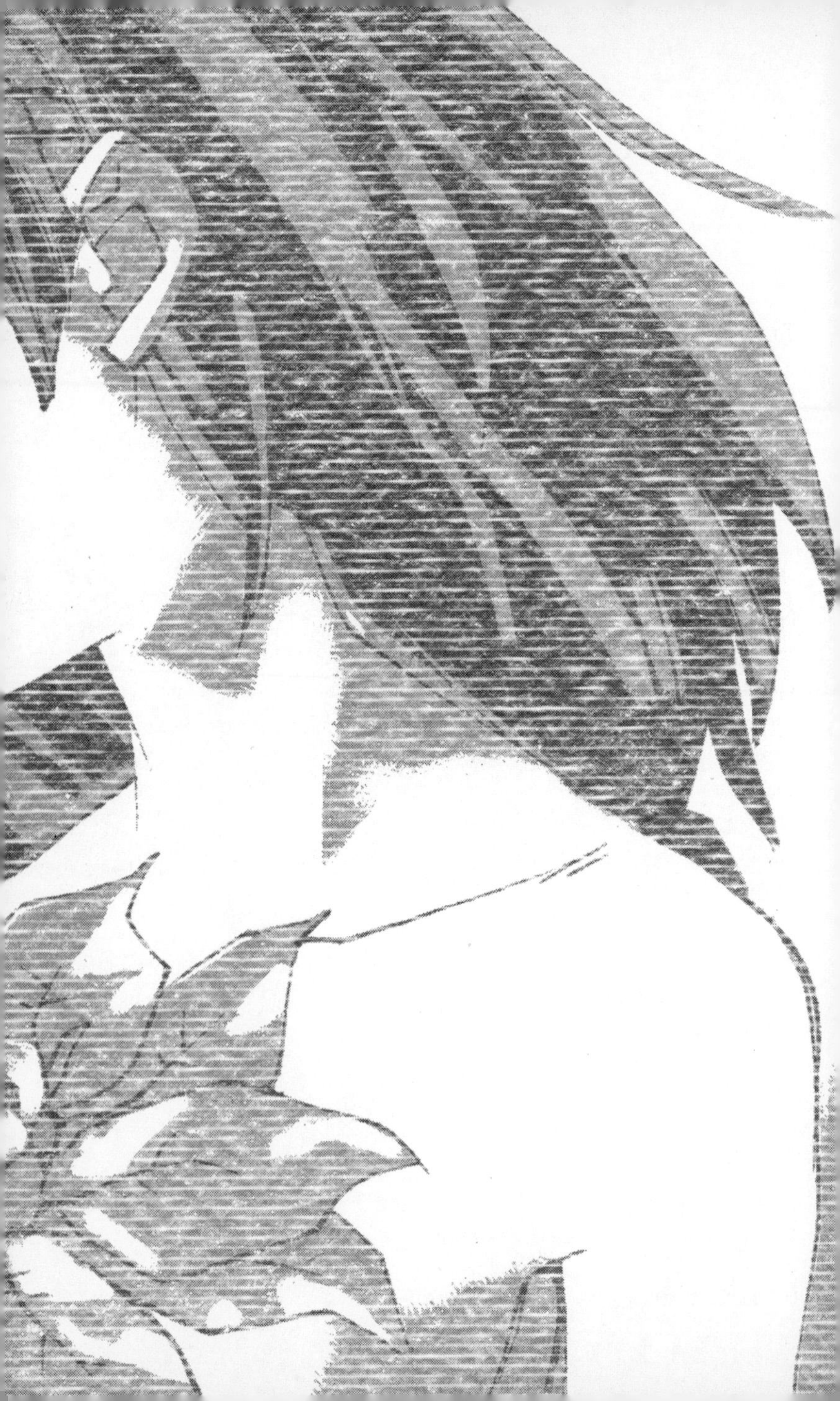

SEVEN SEAS' COMMITMENT TO TRANSLATION AUTHENTICITY

JAPANESE NAME ORDER

To ensure maximum authenticity in Seven Seas' translation of *Boogiepop Returns: VS Imaginator Part 1*, all character names have been kept in their original Japanese name order with family name first and given name second. For copyright reasons, the names of *Boogiepop* creator Kouhei Kadono and illustrator Kouji Ogata appear in standard English name order.

HONORIFICS

In addition to preserving the original Japanese name order, Seven Seas is committed to ensuring that honorifics—polite speech that indicates a person's status or relationship towards another individual—are retained within this book. Politeness is an integral facet of Japanese culture and we believe that maintaining honorifics in our translations helps bring out the same character nuances as seen in the original work.

The following are some of the more common honorifics you may come across while reading this and other books:

-san – The most common of all honorifics, it is an all-purpose suffix that can be used in any situation where politeness is expected. Generally seen as the equivalent to Mr., Miss, Ms., Mrs., etc.

-sama – This suffix is one level higher than "-san" and is used to confer great respect upon an individual.

-dono – Stemming from the word "tono," meaning "lord," "-dono" signifies an even higher level than "-sama," and confers the utmost respect.

-kun – This suffix is commonly used at the end of boys' names to express either familiarity or endearment. It can also be used when addressing someone younger than oneself or of a lower status.

-chan – Another common honorific. This suffix is mainly used to express endearment towards girls, but can also be used when referring to little boys or even pets. Couples are also known to use the term amongst each other to convey a sense of cuteness and intimacy.

Sempai – This title is used towards one's senior or "superior" in a particular group or organization. "Sempai" is most often used in a school setting, where underclassmen refer to upperclassmen as "sempai," though it is also commonly said by employees when addressing fellow employees who hold seniority in the workplace.

Kouhai – This is the exact opposite of "sempai," and is used to refer to underclassmen in school, junior employees at the workplace, etc.

Sensei – Literally meaning "one who has come before," this title is used for teachers, doctors, or masters of any profession or art.

Possibility, or what we refer to as Imagination, is 99% imitation. The real deal is only 1%. The problem is, this 1% is simultaneously referred to as Evil.

— Kirima Seiichi (*VS Imaginator*)

Prelude

On a very cold and snowy day in early March, a girl climbed to the top of our prefectural high school, Shinyo Academy, and proceeded to throw herself off of the roof of the building. Her name was Minahoshi Suiko. She was only seventeen.

"Mariko-san, what do *you* like most?" she asked me abruptly one day, back when she was still alive.

Without putting much thought into it, I gave her the name of a pop star that everyone was listening to.

"Hmm…really?"

"Yeah. He's kinda cool," I said offhandedly.

Suiko-san took a deep breath, faced the setting sun, and began to whistle.

Our school is up in the mountains, and it's a place where most students end up taking the bus to get to or from. On that particular day, Suiko-san and I had decided to walk home together, and we had the streets all to ourselves.

The tune she whistled turned out to be the pop star's most

popular song. Suiko-san was clearly an exceptional whistler. She made the melody seem quite beautiful, to the point that it sounded much, much better than the actual song itself. When she finished, I couldn't help but applaud.

"That was amazing! Suiko, you're *really* good!"

"Not really. If you liked it, it's simply because you already had a predisposition to liking it in the first place."

She was the type of person who said dramatic things like that, and it came to her quite naturally.

"You must have practiced, though. Do you play an instrument?"

"No, just by ear."

"Then you must have perfect pitch or something. That's so awesome! What do you usually listen to?"

"Stuff nobody's ever heard of."

"Like what?"

"Mm, for example," and she took another breath, and began a different piece.

This time, it was more humming than whistling, as if she were a magical instrument that could reproduce any melody in existence.

".......!" I was so stunned just listening to her that I forgot to breathe.

There was simply no comparison to the first song. There was a resonance in my chest, a vibration in my heart that somehow made me feel very sad, all of a sudden. It was a strange melody—both rhythmical and powerful.

When she finished, I couldn't applaud. I was too choked up, with tears welling up in my eyes.

"…What's wrong? Didn't you like it?"

"No…no! It was…it was…uh, I feel sort of embarrassed now. It's like my song was just an imitation of real music…"

"I thought you liked that song?"

"N-no, I think I couldn't have, really. When I heard your song just now, it felt like…this is the first time that I've ever really known that I liked a piece of music. And it didn't have anything to do with what's popular or trendy!" I exclaimed, getting worked up.

"That's nice," Suiko-san said, smiling. She was as beautiful, if not more so, than the song itself. She stood there, backlit by the red light of the evening sky. It was like I was seeing the silhouette of a goddess.

"What song was that?" I asked.

She giggled. "You won't laugh?"

"Why would I?"

"The name of the piece is *Salome*. It's from a ballet."

"What's odd about that?"

"The composer is Ifukube Akira."

"Who?"

"He's most famous for writing the soundtracks to monster movies," Suiko-san said, putting her hand to her mouth, shoulders trembling as she laughed.

This gesture was so feminine that it made my heart beat faster. I thought to myself that I could never laugh that naturally. No, there was nobody else I knew who could laugh so beautifully or as unreservedly as her.

But now she was no longer with us.

I couldn't understand it. Why would a girl like her ever want to kill herself?

They said she didn't even leave a note. We don't know if she had some secret pain that drove her to it, or if she did it just to prove some kind of point.

But I wanted to know. I had to know.

I can't honestly say that the two of us were all that close.

But on those rare occasions when we were alone together, she would always talk openly to me. That was about it, though.

Still, she was without a doubt the most real person I'd ever met up to that point. I can't think of any other way of describing it. Everyone else was just imitating someone else, trying desperately to pretend that it was their true nature. They were all frauds.

So I thought that there must be some meaning behind her suicide.

That's why I'm going to follow her.

Is that imitation too? Probably.

What's sad is that I don't even know if I really loved her. And that's the irony; my life is going to end without me really understanding much of anything.

***

Komiya Mariko stood on the roof of the school, composing her suicide note in her head, but she decided not to write it down.

The sky was dark.

The sun had set a long time ago, and the last traces of light were quickly fading away.

"Suiko-san…"

She looked over the edge of the roof.

Below her, she could still see the white line where Minahoshi Suiko's body had landed. The world around her was almost completely dark, but that line alone seemed to glow, floating upwards.

She swallowed.

Something that Minahoshi Suiko had said to her once popped into her head.

"Mariko-san, there's nothing in this world that is ever truly decided. Birds sometimes fall out of the sky, and sometimes it snows in April. Everything is uncertain, nothing is 'unnatural.'"

I wonder what that meant?

Perhaps I'll understand if I just climb over this fence…!

The white line moved, beckoning to her. It was an illusion, but it seemed too natural to call it that. It made perfect sense to Mariko.

There seemed to be no other logical choice for her doing anything else in life except jumping. The impulse rose up inside her. Her body shook, but not with fear—no, it was excitement.

"Suiko-san…!"

Komiya Mariko grabbed hold of the fence, preparing to climb.

But a voice came from behind her.

"—You wish to follow Minahoshi Suiko? You can't do it that way. It's impossible."

The voice was very strange…like that of a boy or a girl, yet at the same time, neither.

"——?!" Mariko turned around in surprise.

He sat on the other side of the roof, half hidden in darkness. A pipe-shaped black hat half hid his eyes, and he was wrapped in a black cape with a number of rivets attached to it. He wore black lipstick, contrasting with the white of his face.

"If you jump now, you will not end up where she has gone," he said quietly.

"Y-you're…?" Mariko said. She was clearly shaken, but not because she didn't know him. No, she knew all about him. All the girls in school were talking about him.

But for him to be real…?

"It seems you know me. That makes things easier." His left eye narrowed, and the right side of his mouth curled up in a strange, asymmetrical expression.

"W-what do you mean? Why can't I go to her?"

"Simple. You are about to end your life of your own free will. But Minahoshi Suiko did not. If there is such a thing as heaven, you will surely end up in a different place than her." It would be accurate to describe his voice as chilly.

"She did not end her life of her 'own free will?' What does that mean?" Mariko felt as if the ground beneath her feet was crumbling.

"You know my name, don't you? Then you know what I do." He was half shrouded in darkness. It looked as if he were dissolving into thin air.

"Th-then...you?"

"Yes. I am a *shinigami*. Minahoshi Suiko did not kill herself. I...killed her."

"W-why?!"

"Because she was an enemy of the world."

"......!"

"So now what? Do you still wish to die? Unfortunately, I'm afraid I have no intention of killing you. You are not even worth that much."

"B-but...but..." Mariko stuttered, confused. She wasn't sure of anything now.

The enemy of the world? Suiko-san? How? What did that mean?

"Alternatively, I could put it this way. Minahoshi Suiko has not yet reached the next world. Unlike me, she was not 'divided,' but she was equally 'automatic.' But where she is now...I really couldn't tell you."

Mariko couldn't understand anything the cloaked figure was saying.

She hadn't reached the next world?

Reflexively, Mariko looked at the ground below on the other side of the fence. It was now too dark to make out the white line any longer.

It was crazy. Mariko had seen her...seen what used to be her, as the authorities carried her body away under a bloodstained, white shroud. What did it all mean?

"What does it mean, Boogie—?!" Mariko cried out, turning around...but the cloaked figure was gone.

She looked around, but came up with nothing. The darkness was too complete. It was impossible to tell where the mysterious figure in black had gone.

Or perhaps he had never physically been there at all.

"............"

At last, fear welled up in Mariko's heart.

She glanced at the ground below.

But the fence that had seemed so easy to scale a moment ago now seemed as if it were a hundred meters tall.

"Aah..."

"It's impossible."

"You will not end up where she has gone."

"Minahoshi Suiko has not yet reached the next world."

Her legs shook.

"Aaaaah...!"

And Mariko crumbled, falling to the floor. Tear after tear rolled down her face. She couldn't stop them from coming. They were the first tears she'd shed since Minahoshi Suiko had died.

She had been convinced it was better to die than to cry, but now she couldn't hold the tears back.

"I'm sorry. I'm sorry...I'm sorry, I'm sorry, I'm sorry..." she whispered in a slow rhythm, as she rocked herself back and forth. But her tiny voice was faint and was swept away by the wind, and lost in the night.

***

"…………"

The cloaked figure in the black hat watched her from below. Beneath his feet was a white line in the shape of a person.

He went down on his knee, and ran his hand over the line.

"She's certainly not *here* anymore…" he murmured, and stood up. "Are you going to try again? *Imaginator*?"

His black cape flapped furiously in the night wind.

Boogiepop
returns
VS Imaginator Part 1

SIGNS

I

If you wish to be good, then do not have
dealings with the future. In most cases,
that only leads to distortion.

—Kirima Seiichi (*VS Imaginator*)

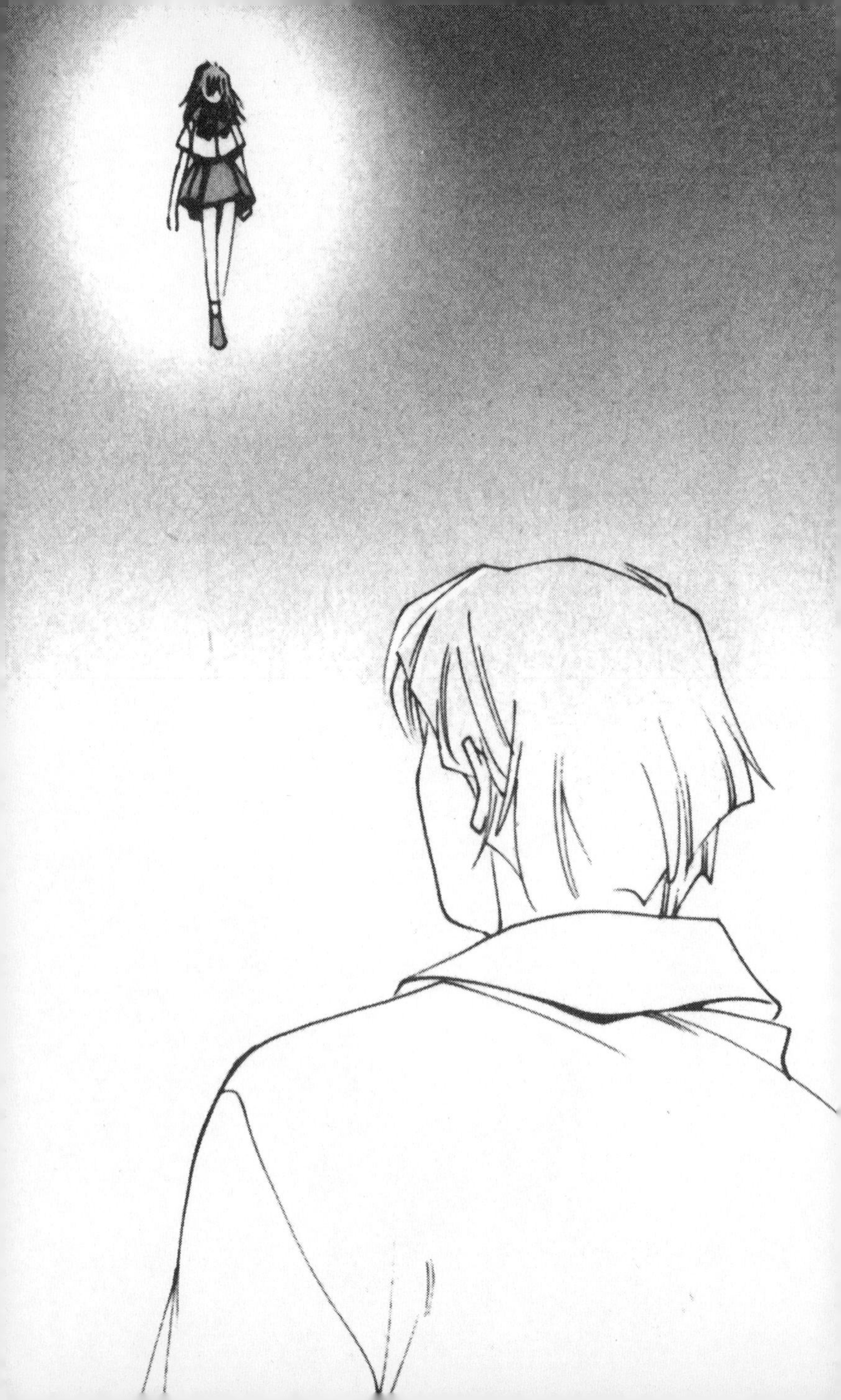

"**S**ometimes I wake up in the middle of the night," she said. Her name was Nakadai Sawako, and her cheekbones stood out ever so slightly. But her face was very pale, and to Asukai Jin, she looked like a dried-up, withered bouquet inside an oversized jacket.

"Hmm," he said.

"I know it's cliché, but I feel like something's sitting on my chest, looking at me. But when I open my eyes…"

"There's nothing there?"

"Yes. I mean, I know it's a dream, but…I have it over and over again. So…"

Sawako's shoulders trembled. In her hair, there were still lingering traces of a two-month-old perm, but she wasn't one to take care of herself, and she had obviously paid little attention to it since then. And understandably so—there were only four more months left until her entrance exam. Like so many girls, she would make an appointment to have her hair straightened just before the big day, and then strive to take good care of it in order to make a good impression at the interview, but at the moment, she simply didn't have the time to care.

"This…'shadow'…" Asukai said, interrupting her. "Has it said anything to you?"

She looked up at him, surprised. "Yes! Yes, it has. How did you know?"

Ignoring her question, he asked another, "What did it say? Do you remember?"

"N-no, I…"

"You can't remember at all?"

"Right," she nodded.

The cram school was designed to squeeze a large number of people into a very small space to begin with, and the guidance office was hidden in a corner of the building. It was about the size of a prison's solitary confinement cell. And the two of them were all alone in the tiny room.

There was only one window—a long, thin, vertical slit in the wall, through which a single ray of light penetrated. The light was red. It was already evening.

"Hmm…" Asukai said again, shutting his mouth and looking down at the girl's chest.

'…She has no roots,' he thought. 'Very few leaves…only the buds are large, and they're almost breaking the stem…'

Sawako grew uncomfortable in the silence, and began locking her fingers together on her knees.

"Um, Asukai-sensei…?"

"…………"

He didn't respond.

He had a pointed chin and a thin face with a serene beauty to it. He was not much older than Sawako, just past twenty. He was a student at a public university, but he taught art part time at this cram school. And he had taken over the highly unpopular position of guidance counselor.

"…………"

She looked up at him timidly. At some point, he'd taken his eyes off her and was staring out the window.

"I-I'm sorry, this all must sound crazy…" Sawako whispered, unable to stand it any longer.

Quietly, Asukai said, "As a teacher, I know I'm not supposed to say this. But maybe you should try not to take exams so seriously."

"What do you mean?"

"Getting into the best university isn't going to relieve you of your worries…or guarantee your future," he continued, almost like he was reading some inspirational pamphlet. "I know a lot of people who slaved away, got into college, and then had no idea what to do once they were there. All they'd ever done was study, and they didn't know how to just let go and enjoy themselves. So they'd go off to try and pass the civil servants exam or something. They were just pointlessly limiting their options for a…I dunno, a decent future. They meet the person they were supposed to fall in love with, but they don't recognize how valuable they are, and before they realize it, they wind up missing out on the most important things in life.

"They're college students, but they can't shake the exam student mentality. And very few people can pass on their first try. Most people fail. They become *ronin*. They fritter away their precious youth, and end up, frankly, really screwed up because of it."

She just sat there listening, wide-eyed.

"You see?" Asukai asked, turning towards her.

"Um, not…"

"You *already know* this, don't you? But you're doing your very best *not to think about it*. But doing your best and avoiding the truth…they're two different things. We can't tell you not to overdo it, though. The only way to actually pass these tests…*is* to overdo it. But it's important not to overburden you with excessive, and frankly, unrealistic expectations. I know you've heard this all before, but getting into college is not your whole life. That dream about the shadow is a sign that you're unconsciously resisting the notion of getting into college. I just think you need to relax a bit."

"O-okay," she nodded obediently. "But…but still…"

"Yeah. That's why you need to work at it. It isn't a bad thing to want to go to college. It's not like it's an impossible dream, either. But it just isn't healthy to get obsessed with it, you know? At this rate, you're just going to get overwhelmed by the pressure and be in no condition to actually sit there and take the test."

"I…I think I understand," Sawako said meekly.

'…The bud relaxed a little,' Asukai thought. 'If she could

just sprout a few more leaves…not that it would take care of all of her problems, but it would be a start.'

He was looking at her chest again.

He could see something there.

Nobody else could see it, including the girl herself.

After that, they spoke in more concrete terms about how they should go about handling her problem subjects.

"—Thank you very much!" she yelled as she stood up twenty minutes later.

"Your effort is genuine. All you have to do is just stay calm, and keep moving forward."

"Okay. And thanks, Sensei," she started. "I feel much better now. Say, did you ever have some sort of training? Like as a therapist or counselor?"

"Not really."

"Maybe you should consider a new career. You're really smart and good looking too." Asukai gave her an awkward smile, and she slapped her hand over her mouth. "Ah! Sorry! I didn't mean to be rude…!"

"I'll think about," he chuckled. "They do say you can't make a living painting."

As she was about to leave, Sawako suddenly turned back, remembering something. "Oh, right! Sensei, have you heard the phrase 'Sometimes it snows in April'?"

"W-what?" Asukai said, shocked.

"That's the only thing I remember from my dream. Oh, but it's probably not important. Good-bye!" she said brightly as she exited—her gloomy exterior having finally been shed.

"Sometimes…it snows in April?"

For some reason, those words made something stir inside Asukai.

***

When Asukai Jin thought about his strange ability to see the flaws in people's hearts, he always remembered Saint-Exupery's *The Little Prince*. He had read it when he was three or four years old, but he remembered one line from it that went something like, "The reason this child was beautiful was because he had a rose within his heart."

He felt as if that image had been carved into his psyche and left a lasting impression on him.

His eyes could see a single plant growing from every person's chest. The variety of plant in his vision varied, and they came in all sorts of shapes and sizes, but the problem was not the variety of plant, but with the very fact that in every vision, there was some part missing.

Perhaps there was no flower. Or no leaves. No stem. Or, like this girl, no roots. He had never once seen a person that carried a complete plant within their chest.

There was always a flaw.

So, his 'advice' was simply to say whatever was needed to compensate for that flaw. If there were no roots, all he had to do was tell them to have more confidence. Everyone would be satisfied by that, and recover their good cheer.

His job at the cram school finished, he walked back to his apartment along a bustling shopping street. He couldn't help but notice the flaws on everyone's chests.

It annoyed him, occasionally.

Human effort was entirely devoted to making up for this flaw. He knew this. But he also knew that what they lacked was never in them to begin with, and it was something that could never be obtained.

He had looked at his own chest before, but he could find nothing there. Presumably, he was lacking something also, and it was that missing item that was making him so unhappy. Unfortunately, there was no way for him to replace it either.

"…So that's why *I* said…"

"…What the…?"

"…Hahaha! That's so *dumb*…"

Drunks, young people, old people, males, females…they all passed him by. None of them ever thought that they were missing flowers or roots.

(They're happier *not* knowing…)

Since he was very young, he had always felt isolated.

Perhaps he always would.

"—Oh, look! Snow!"

"Wow! It's so pretty!"

Everyone around him was cheering at the sky, so Asukai felt obligated to look up as well.

Something white was falling out of the night sky.

(I do like snow…)

Snow turned everything white. It was one of his favorite things. Perhaps because flowers never bloomed beneath it. He could go about his business without thinking about anything else…or so he felt.

But when he looked happily up at the sky, his expression suddenly froze.

There was a girl standing in the fifth story window of a nearby building.

Her feet were on the window ledge, her body all the way outside, getting ready to jump.

As he stared up at her, their eyes met.

She smiled slightly with her eyes. Then…

"No…!" Asukai tried to shout, but she flung her body outward into the open air.

Reflexively, Asukai ran towards her.

But his feet went out from under him, and he fell awkwardly.

He hurriedly scrambled back to his feet, but as he looked up again, he saw something impossible.

"Heh heh heh."

The girl was floating in mid-air, laughing.

But there was something unique about her smile. Her mouth was closed in a straight line, and her eyes alone smiled, sweet and enchanting.

She was frozen in mid-air, about to fall, but not moving at all.

"Hunh…?" he wondered.

"Hey, wake up! You're in the way," snarled a group of drunks, brushing past him.

"D-do you see that?" Asukai asked, pointing at the girl.

None of them paid much attention. "What are you talking about?"

"You've had too much to drink!"

They were looking where he was pointing, but none of them could see her.

(W-what on earth…?)

He stood up, looking up at her, stunned.

Now that he looked carefully, he could tell that she was actually falling, just very, very slowly. Her tangled hair was moving, swaying.

"Heheheh."

Those laughing eyes drank in the light like holes in the sky.

"It isn't much fun to see things nobody else can, is it, Asukai-sensei?" he heard her whisper in his ear.

"How…?"

"I know exactly how you feel. I used to be the same."

Asukai stumbled over, until he was directly below the falling girl.

"Th-then you…"

"Just like your extra sensory perception, I can see people's deaths."

Her expression never changed—that tightly closed mouth never moved. It was as if time around her moved at a snail's pace.

"Deaths?"

"To be more accurate, I can see the energy field generated by all living things just before they burn themselves out." She laughed again. "I represent a possibility in which people are able to manipulate death. My purpose is to recreate the world in that fashion, which makes me an enemy of the current world. Even in spring, I bring cold. I make it snow in April."

"Er…"

"Will you help me with my work, Asukai-sensei?"

"What…? What are you talking about? Who are you?!" he shouted.

The people around him looked at him suspiciously. To them, he was shouting at empty space. They must have thought him plastered beyond his limit or tripped out on drugs.

In the air above him, the girl replied, "My enemies call me the *Imaginator*."

And she vanished.

"W-wait!" he cried, reaching out towards her, but his fingers only brushed empty air.

"…………"

He was amazed, but then his shoulders slumped in disappointment. He thought to himself that he had finally gone completely insane. Seeing things. It was obvious—and then he glanced at his feet, and almost shouted.

The falling snow had piled up all around, except at his feet, where a small patch of pavement was left exposed.

It was like a shadow puppet in the shape of a girl falling from the sky.

***

When Asukai got back to his apartment, a girl poked her head out of the window of the room next door as if she'd been waiting for him.

"—There you are! Welcome back!" She said brightly. She was Kinukawa Kotoe, the apartment owner's daughter, and also his cousin. Kotoe had talked her parents into letting her use one of the empty rooms as a study. Her own house was about a minute's walk away.

"Wh-what is it?" he said blankly, still a little out of it.

"Jin-niisan, did you eat yet? I just made some stew; thought you might like some."

"Um, yeah…thanks."

"Cool! I'll bring it over in a minute!" She ducked back into the room.

Kotoe was always like this. Asukai's father had died two years before, and he was renting a room in his uncle's apartment building. But that was the extent of their involvement. Asukai had a scholarship covering his university's tuition, but his art supplies, living expenses and rent all had to be covered by the money he made from his meager cram school salary. About the only liberty he had taken was to rent the room without a guarantor, but Kotoe had taken it upon herself to look after him.

Seeing Kotoe up and in her usual cheerful mood actually helped Asukai to calm his nerves a little.

(Whether that was an illusion or not, it's not like I've never seen anything that outright bizarre before...)

If he kept his cool, he could deal with this, just like he had all along.

He entered his apartment, splashed his face a few times with water from his bathroom sink, and turned to find Kotoe coming in with a big pot in her hands.

"Okay! Today's dinner is especially good, if I do say so myself!"

She set the table briskly, as if this were her own room, and placed a steaming hot bowl in front of a slightly embarrassed Asukai.

"It does look good. Thanks."

"Jin-niisan, you look kinda tired. Everything okay?"

"Yeah...it's just a busy time of year. My students are all feeling it, and I catch it from them."

"That sucks."

"It's not like you won't be going through the same thing next year yourself."

Kotoe was a second year student at a local prefectural school called Shinyo Academy.

"Yeah, well...I dunno if I'm goin' to college..."

She glanced up at him.

"Or maybe...I just could go to your cram school and you could teach me..."

"When did you decide to go to art school? I teach art history and design, you know."

"But you also do counseling? I could use some of that…"

"We can do that here anytime for free. No reason to sign up where I work."

"Really?" Kotoe beamed.

"But the kids I counsel are all very serious people. Not so sure about you…" he teased, winking.

"That's so mean! Like you think I'm some sort of airhead!" she said, puffing out her cheeks and pouting. But she couldn't keep it up, and soon they were both laughing.

Kotoe let out a little sigh. "I guess I do come across like that…"

"And thank god you do. You're better off *not* needing my help," Asukai said sincerely, lowering his spoon.

"Mm?"

"I think people need to work their way through their own problems. And with the tests…I'm a cram school teacher, so there's a lot I can't say. I can't tell them they don't need to go to college…even if they really shouldn't be trying…"

He glanced over at Kotoe's chest.

She had no 'flower.'

What she did have was a bountiful amount of leaves, which were the domain of kindness and warmth, and her stem and roots were equally secure. But there was no flower to be found.

Kotoe was a good girl.

She wasn't bad looking. Her parents owned several apartment

buildings, and were obviously rich. There was no reason at all for her to be unhappy.

But deep in her heart, she wondered, 'Why have I never come across anything definitively radiant?' Sometimes she would see a really ordinary, average person who was completely passionate about some insignificant thing. This would devastate her—she would be terribly jealous of them.

But there was nothing she could do about it.

She 'lacked' that passion, and she would never have it.

"Jin-niisan, you just need to chill." Never in her wildest dreams able to guess what he was looking at, Kotoe tried using her usual hip slang to cheer him up. "You spend way too much time stressing over other people. You've gotta at least try to make things a little easier on yourself, you know." She nodded, oddly forceful.

"Th-thanks. But now I don't know which of us is getting counseled," Asukai grinned.

"Nothing is futile! There is always a path...even if it's towards something that doesn't exist yet," she proclaimed.

"Um...yeah, I guess," Asukai nodded, but with no conviction. "I wish I could think that..."

"But that path may be a trifle...cruel...it might even go against all that this world deems just," her voice was so certain; it seemed almost scornful.

"...Huh?" Asukai looked up. That didn't sound like something Kotoe would say.

He froze.

The vision at her chest had vanished.

It had been there just a moment before, but now he could see nothing.

And her expression—her mouth was closed in a straight line, her eyes alone sparkling, laughing—

"Wh-who are you?!" Asukai cried out, leaping to his feet.

"Relax. *I am only borrowing her body…temporarily,*" the girl with Kotoe's face whispered.

"Wh-what?!"

"This girl's psyche *is not capable of becoming my vessel,*" she said quietly. "I must leave her in a moment."

"You weren't a delusion…you're a ghost?"

"No…not a ghost," she said, standing to face him. "To be completely accurate, I am a 'hypothetical possibility given substance.' But for your feeble mind, consider me 'a glimpse of the future.'"

She reached towards Asukai's forehead.

She stroked it gently with both hands.

"Asukai-sensei, don't you feel it's time you…*did* something?"

"About what?"

"The flaws found in human hearts."

Her soft, gentle fingertips massaged Asukai's face, firmly.

He moaned. The sensation was sweet and hard to resist.

"What do you think your flaw is, Asukai-sensei?"

"………?!"

"You lack a 'calling.'" Her voice was peaceful, yet firm.

"...Eh?"

"Let me show you a little glimpse of the future."

She pulled his face towards hers, arched her back, and placed her thin lips upon his.

Instantly, *something* opened in Asukai's head.

A torrent of images cascaded past him.

"Ah...aaauuughhhhhh!" he screamed, forcing her away.

She never flinched, simply staggered once and then stared back at him again.

"Hahh...hahh..." Asukai gasped for breath. "Wh-what was that...that spectacle?"

"Your 'calling,' Asukai-sensei."

"L-like hell! I would never do something like *that*!"

"The choice is yours. But you *are capable of it*. Nothing will change the truth of that. The reason for your birth is *there*...and only there."

"Shut up! What...what are you, some sort of demon?! I...I..." he wheezed, unable to find the words.

"Am I tempting you? No. That's not my intent. It's up to you to decide." Her eyes alone laughed. "But, Asukai-sensei, remember this. Birds do fall from the sky, and sometimes it does snow in April."

"Get away!"

Asukai flung the contents of his stew bowl at her.

She made no effort to dodge, but simply stood there and took it.

A moment later there was a scream. "Ow! Wh-what the

heck?!"

Asukai gasped.

Kotoe was back.

"A-are you…"

"Why…why am I…? Gross!!!" Kotoe said, confused; no idea what was going on. Her memories didn't match up.

Asukai wiped her face off with a towel, trying to keep his body from shaking.

(…What did she call herself? The Imaginator…?)

**

He might well be going crazy, but that was no reason to skip work. Asukai was at the cram school again, speaking with yet another student.

"I can't do this anymore. It's not for me. Like, in the middle of the night, I can be taking notes…and my hands just start shaking," the girl said, nodding to herself, over and over.

There was no stem in the girl's 'vision.' She had roots, but they connected directly into the leaves and base of the flower.

"You need a change," he answered, but Asukai knew it was useless. This girl was afraid that nothing in her being was ever secure. No matter how often she tried something new, her anxiety would always be there. Whether she passed the exam or not, nothing would change.

"What should I do?"

"Take a break, do whatever you like. Or change the way you

study. You've got a good memory, don't you?"

People without stems were good at stuffing things in. They were unable to turn that knowledge and experience into anything, to nurture it or let it grow. They could put in as much as they liked, but it would just pile up, never changing, never rotting.

"I suppose so…"

"Then spend one week concentrating on solving equations. Halve the number of things to memorize."

"Ah…b-but…" She hesitated…but with a clear goal placed in front of her, her eyes shone. Her type had no conscious goals of their own, so they tended to relax if you gave them one. "Will that work?"

"I'm sure you can do it. Your percentile's been going up," Asukai replied. He wanted to add, 'that won't save you, though…' but he let the words die in his throat. It was futile.

"Okay! I'll try it. Sensei, thank you so much!"

"You're the one who has to do the work."

"No, it's because you really know how to help people. Everyone says so! Seems such a shame to waste that kind of talent on a cram school."

"Hey, now."

"Asukai-sensei, I think you were meant to do something much more important. Yeah, you probably were."

"Hmm…who knows?"

"You are capable of it. Nothing will change the truth of that."

"I just can't get into it," the boy said, sullenly.

"Hmm…your first results were pretty good, but they haven't improved at all," Asukai looked up from the boy's file, and checked the vision at his chest.

No leaves.

This type took no pleasure in life. Since his flower and stem were doing pretty well, he was fully capable of better things, but everything he tried dried up around him.

"I know I gotta do better…"

"Studying bores you, right?" Asukai said bluntly and to the point.

The boy nodded, wryly. "Basically."

"You know why?" Asukai's tone changed, becoming sort of chummy.

"Nope."

"'Cause it's boring. What other reason is there?" he grinned. This was all part of the performance.

"Well, shit, if you put it that way…" the boy said, grinning back. Anyone else would lose their motivation if their teacher talked to them like this, but with this type there was no risk of that.

"Look, I know it's tedious as hell. And you're expected to do whatever us teachers tell you to do…so how's that ever gonna be fun? All we're doing is just following some stupid rulebook anyway."

"Ha ha ha!"

"When you get down to it, passing tests is a matter of understanding the system. You know why I can work part time here, right? It's not like I've got a teaching license or anything."

"Well...you got experience, right?"

"Yep. Few years ago, just like you, I was trying to pass these exams. I kept hitting all these brick walls and I was just banging my head trying to figure out an easy way to pass. Now, I make a living passing on all those little tricks I figured out."

"Ah ha! I get ya."

"See? Studying has some use after all."

"Not just for getting into college, you mean?"

"Exactly. These days, getting into a good college doesn't even mean that much. You only go because you *have* to go. Still, that's no reason to kill yourself studying. But if you look at it as training...I don't know what it is you want to be, but whatever it is, you're gonna have to develop a few tricks—a few techniques. Think of all this as, like, a simulation. No, think of it like a game. There aren't that many other times in your life where society itself and all of the people around you will just up and support you, but this is one of those times. It gives you the freedom to experiment."

Personally, Asukai just thought he was talking crap, but the boy sitting across from him was visibly happier.

"Never thought of it that way..."

"Yeah, just think of the test itself as just another chance to gather data and experiment."

"Right..."

"But in that sense, you've got a little catching up to do. On these results, you'll end up in a second rate school. That'd suck, right? Waste of a good opportunity."

This was a little logical slight of hand, but the boy never noticed.

People with no leaves feel like they aren't connected to the world around them. No matter what they do, they can never feel peace of mind when they are around other people. To compensate, they pretty much lose themselves in methodology. They know all sorts of approaches to things and all sorts of tricks, but all they're doing is trying to make up for an inability to communicate with others.

Being nice to them, praising them…it's all useless. Staying firmly on a practical ground worked best.

But the end result of all of their tricks only served to drive them even further into isolation. Since nobody else needed these tricks, they couldn't understand how much work went into them. Those of the same type were especially cruel—if they happened to be using different methodologies.

None of them would ever find an 'ally.'

"Okay, I'll try it out." Drawn along by Asukai's friendly manner, the boy was now completely comfortable.

"You've still got plenty of time," Asukai nodded. He didn't dare add, 'But all your efforts and memories will never be appreciated by anyone else.' That revelation would only be utterly futile.

"But, Sensei," the boy asked. "What are you planning on

doing when you get out of college?"

"Dunno. Probably try and make a living painting."

"Seems like a waste, man. You ought to start your own business, do something big. Seriously." His eyes were serious, no sense of the mocking that this type so often engaged in.

"Maybe."

"You lack a 'calling.'"

"I keep having this dream over and over."

"What kind?"

"Um, Sensei…have you ever heard the phrase 'Sometimes it snows in April'?"

"Uh…n-no, can't say that I have. W-why?"

"In the dream, someone—I don't know who—keeps saying that to me. When I hear those words, I just don't care about anything anymore. This stupid test, this ugly world—they just don't matter to me. Not anymore."

"…………"

"But whoever it is, they are a little too nice…and that's sort of scary. When I wake up, it feels like someone just threw a bucket of cold water in my face. *Brrr*…"

"…………"

"And after I have that dream, I can't do anything. I had one the day before the last practice test, and I couldn't figure out a single problem."

"…………"

"Sensei, is there something wrong with me?"

"............."

"Sensei? Uh, Asukai-sensei?"

"—Ah! Oh, uh, hmm?"

"Something wrong?"

"Oh, no. It's nothing."

***

When the last student left, Asukai tried several times to sketch *that face*.

Unfortunately, he couldn't draw it well enough, and he crumpled up all of his attempted pages and flung them into the corner of the counseling office, missing the wastebasket.

Afterwards, he knelt down to collect them all and wondered to himself, "What the hell am I doing...?"

He sighed, balled up the failed sketches as tightly as he could, and buried them deep within the office wastebasket.

***

Several days passed like this, repeating the same answers over and over for an endless progression of identical worries, occasionally encountering the phrase "Sometimes it snows in April" among them.

Then one day, as he walked along the streets after work, he heard a groan from a back alley.

"Unh…unh…s-somebody…" he heard, faintly.

"…?" He turned off the main road, heading towards the voice.

"Please…somebody…" It sounded like a girl's voice and in great pain, barely gasping out the words.

"Is somebody there?" Asukai called out. There was no answer.

He moved deeper into the alley, and found a girl slumped against the cul de sac.

"Unhhhhhhhhh," she groaned.

"What's the matter?" Asukai asked as he went over to her, and placed his hand upon her back.

Instantly, his hand was flung off.

The girl sprang up like a jack-in-the-box, launching herself towards him, and slamming his back against the wall. "Don't move," she snarled, with sudden menace. There was a carving knife in her hand.

"You're…" Asukai looked at her face. She was very, very thin, like a skeleton. It was painful to look at her. Her hair was a brittle and matted mess, not at all that of a young girl.

"Heh…heh…that was stupid of you, Asukai-sensei. Even this country's pretty dangerous these days. I knew a sap like you would fall for it……!" she sneered, breathing ragged.

"You were after me…? Imazaki Shizuko, isn't it? You were in my spring course, weren't you?"

She had come to him for counseling once.

"Heh…heh…I'm surprised you remembered." She was gasping for breath. Her eyes were red, bloodshot. It was clear she was on something, presumably some sort of chemical. "But it ain't gonna get you off. Give me all the money you got."

"To buy drugs…? What happened to you? You were such a good student…"

"My dad got arrested for tax evasion or something! Made everything so futile! But what do you care?! Just hand it over!!!" The girl screamed, hysterical.

"………" Asukai looked at the tip of the knife. It was shaking. Her grip on it was so tight she couldn't keep it pointed at him. It would be easy to dodge it.

But he suddenly felt a turmoil of emotion welling up inside him.

Everything seemed so ridiculous—directionless anger abruptly gushed forth from deep within his heart.

"No," he said, crisply, before he even realized it.

"What?" The girl said, looking even fiercer.

"Go ahead and kill me," Asukai spat.

"I'm serious!"

"So am I!" he roared. "You think you can escape by taking drugs? That doesn't do any good! No matter how high you get, there's no saving us!"

"Sh-shut up! You're just scared!" The girl moved the knife closer, touching Asukai's throat.

"Try it!" he yelled, and she put her anger into it, pushing forward.

The knife slipped past, his skin sliced open, and blood came out. She had missed his jugular by a hair's breadth, and he had narrowly escaped death, but Asukai was unaware of this.

The girl toppled over. She didn't have the strength left to keep her footing.

A number of little packets spilled out of her pocket onto the ground—little packets of drugs.

"——!" Asukai frowned down at them. This was hardly for her personal use. With this quantity, there was no reason for her to be trying to mug people. Which meant…

"…Exactly. These are for other people," the girl said, rising slowly to her feet—no, this was no longer the same girl.

Her eyes were laughing, but she had no expression.

"Y-you again," Asukai glared at the thing inhabiting the girl, ignoring the blood dripping from his neck.

"Just to be clear, I took over only a few seconds ago. Most of your encounter was of her own free will," she said coldly. "*If* you can call that free will. It's not like she wanted to do it. She's a girl. If she needed money, there are faster and safer ways for her to get it. But once her body's been torn to pieces like this, those options vanish."

"Shut up!" Despite the fact that the girl had tried to stab him, hearing her insulted made him furious.

"Do you know what these drugs are for, Asukai-sensei?"

The thing inhabiting the girl's body pointed at the ground.

"She was selling them?"

"Exactly. The dosage is too weak for her now—it's beginner's strength. If she wanted more drugs for herself, she had to sell these to other people. That's what they told her. But she couldn't bring herself to ever do that."

She pointed towards her chest.

"Such a *sad* story. Didn't want to make any more people like her, but what else could she do? So she asked you, the only person she could ever remember being nice to her."

"………"

"But, Asukai-sensei, either way, this girl was finished."

"What do you mean?"

"The drugs have destroyed her body. She won't last out the month. She's going to die. Futile, pitiful, miserable and sad," she sneered.

"………"

"But you might be able to do something," she said, picking up the knife, and stabbing it deep into her own neck.

"____!"

For a second, the girl's blood sprayed out, filling the air; and then she fell over.

"Aiiieeeee!" There was a scream.

At the end of the alley, a woman walking by had seen this. She quickly ran away.

Asukai rushed over to the girl.

She was gasping. Her face was back to normal. *She* was gone.

"Shit…!" Asukai pushed his handkerchief against the girl's wound, but half her blood had already emptied out of her in a massive geyser.

Eyes hollow, the girl whispered, "……it………t…"

Asukai leaned close, putting his ear to her lips.

"…mn it, damn it, damn it," she swore. Cursing everything in the world. "Damn it, damn it, damn it, damn it, damn it, damn it, da—!"

Asukai stared down at the girl. She had no choice but to stay angry until the very end.

He grit his teeth, and put his hand on her chest.

It was so much easier than he'd thought.

***

"Let me get this straight…moments after she assaulted you, she suddenly stabbed herself in the throat? This is your story?" The detective asked. He was speaking to the key witness, who had stayed by the side of the body until the patrol cars arrived.

"Yes," Asukai said instantly. There was a bandage around his neck, applied by the doctor at the police hospital.

"You say you knew this girl?"

"Yes. Her name is Imazaki Shizuko. She's about eighteen. I don't know her address, but it's probably still in the files at the cram school. I taught her last spring." He answered smoothly, without faltering. No emotion.

"Did she have something against you? Any idea what?"

"Maybe. She came to me for counseling, but I guess I didn't help her much."

"Well, from what we've been able to ascertain, her family

situation was at the root of it," the detective admitted. He'd decided Asukai's calm responses proved his innocence. "She had reason enough to kill herself."

"Suicide?"

"Yeah. She wouldn't have lasted much longer anyway. The drugs had wrecked her system. The way she died was comparatively pain-free. Overdosing's a nasty way to go. Truth is…we'd had our eyes on her for dealing for a while now. I can tell you that she wasn't much good at it. Heart wasn't in it."

"You knew about her?"

"She was low level for another pusher that we're after, but the big man's still hasn't shown his face."

'You knew, but didn't save her?!' Asukai's poker face hid this thought perfectly.

"You'll be free to go soon. We've got a witness, so we know you didn't kill her. Soon as we wrap things up here, you can leave."

"Thank you," Asukai bowed his head.

The investigation was over soon enough, and he signed and stamped his statement as directed. Asukai rose to leave.

"Oh, Asukai-san…this is just my personal question, but…" the detective started.

"What?"

"While she was dying, did you say something to her?"

"What do you mean?"

"I don't mean anything. Just that girl, dying that way…her face was awfully peaceful. Like the thorns in her heart had all been plucked away. If something you said put her mind at ease, then you must be one hell of a teacher." The aging detective nodded keenly.

"Sorry, I…I didn't say anything," Asukai replied quietly, and left the room.

***

Soon, Asukai found himself walking through the evening streets again.

For every alley he found, he stopped, and peered down it looking for some sort of sign. His eyes never missed a thing, like the eyes of a hawk searching for its next target.

Then he heard a sound, like something falling over. Like the girl's moans, the sound was so faint nobody else around even noticed.

"_____"

But he turned instantly, and went down the alley towards the sound's origin.

He found some people there. Seven in all—six boys and a girl.

Something was clearly going on—the girl's clothes were torn, her naked and vulnerable upper body exposed. Five of the boys stood around her, reaching towards her. One stood to the side, dazed, blood running from his mouth.

"Well, *this* is easy to figure out!" Asukai's voice boomed.

All the boys spun towards him.

"—! Wh-who are you?!"

"Just to make sure, I'd better ask. You there," Asukai pointed to the odd boy out, the one who'd clearly been beaten. "Do you want to save this girl?"

The confidence in Asukai's voice brought the boy out of his daze. He quickly nodded, "Y-yes."

"Then take her and run!" Asukai said, walking straight through the boys, taking the girl's arm, and pulling her out.

"Hey!" The boys said, lurching towards Asukai.

"Hmph," he snorted, and *did something* to one of them, too fast for anyone to see.

The boy fell over backwards.

"——?!"

The others shrank backwards, surprised. Asukai pushed the unresisting girl towards the bleeding boy. "Go! Get out of here!!"

"Th-thank you," the boy mumbled, scrambling away. He grabbed the girl's hand, and ran.

"Wait!" the others shouted, but when they tried to follow, they found Asukai between them.

"You wait," he said, a fearless smile on his face.

"Oh, yeah?!" They shouted, pulling knives from their pockets.

Asukai didn't bat an eyelash at the blades. "I've got no grudge against you," he said. "But I need a few more samples."

***

One minute later—

Everyone else was sprawled on the ground. Only one of the boy thugs was still standing.

Strangely enough, all of their injuries were caused by each other's knives.

"Ah…ahhhh…" the last boy moaned, his teeth chattering together. Asukai came over to him, waving his right hand over his chest.

"Wh-wh-wh-what did you do to them?"

"You wouldn't understand. But I haven't hurt them. I've given them happiness."

His words, his calm, scared the boy more than anything else in his short life.

"Wh-what the hell are you?"

"Mm? Let's see…what was that name?" Asukai looked behind him.

The girl hanging in the sky above him replied, "Imaginator!"

"Right…*that*," Asukai grinned…and his right hand snapped out towards the boy.

There was a muffled scream.

II

*You can fall in love if you like.
All I can do...is pray it does
not destroy you both.*

—**Kirima Seiichi (*VS Imaginator*)**

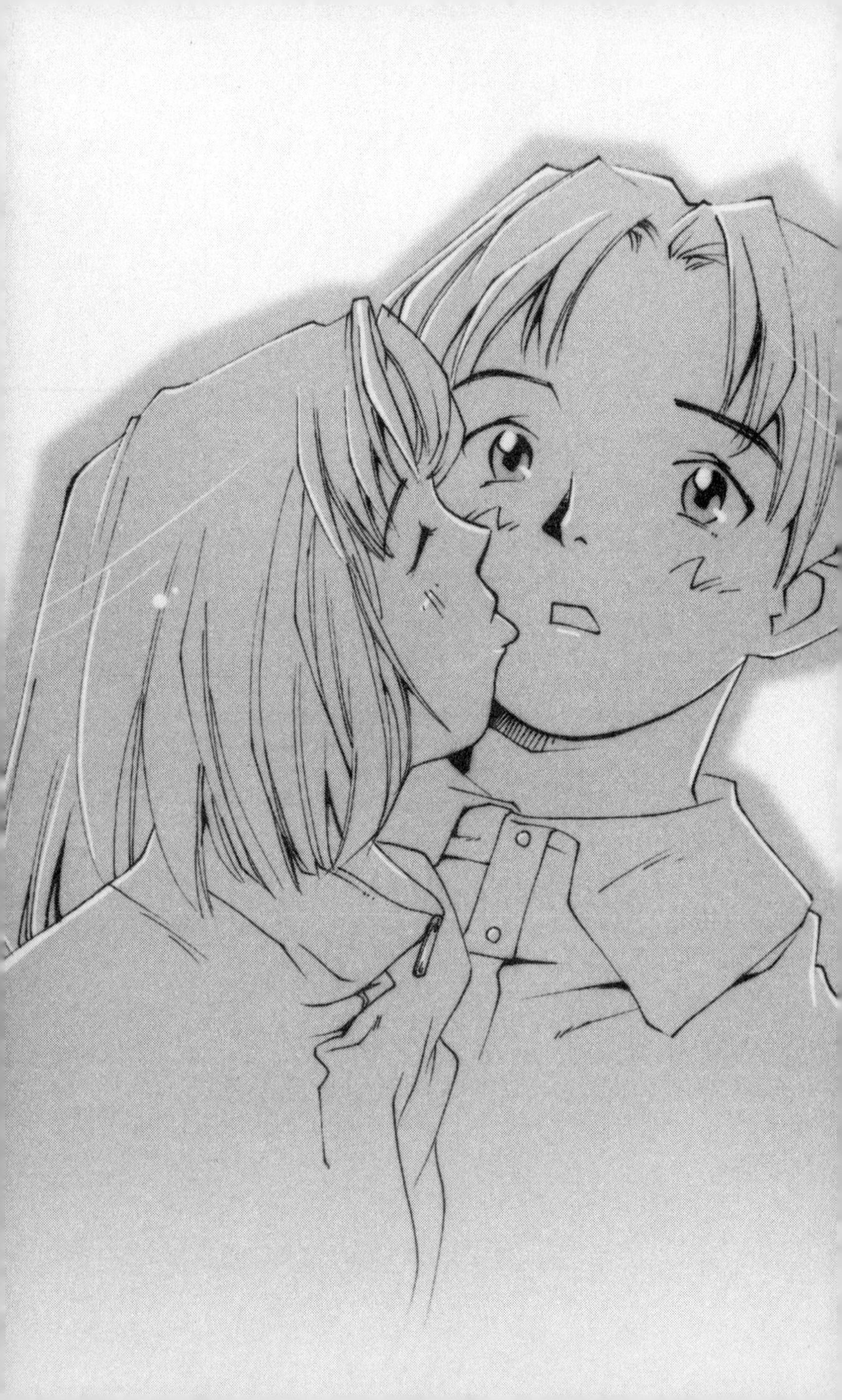

Her name was Orihata Aya.

She had big striking eyes, with large pupils—though, they almost never looked at you directly. Very beautiful, but an incredibly reckless personality, and she always spoke in a very terse fashion. She was the same age as me, which is, well, fifteen, but there was a sort of sobriety about her that most adults never managed to develop.

"Masaki, why are interested in me?"

"Um, I just thought we could...I dunno, be friends, you know?"

"You want me?"

"Hunh?!"

"Do you want to have sex with me?"

"Hey, Orihata—!"

"We can if you want to."

"............"

Yeah, many of our conversations were a lot like this.

She seemed like she didn't even have friends at her school, and until she met me, I had my own doubts whether she'd ever had a normal conversation before.

Oh, right...my name's Taniguchi Masaki, and as you can probably guess, Orihata and I...we're complete opposites. It's funny, though; Orihata and I met in the most messed up kind of way.

At the time, I had just returned to Japan to get ready for high school after having lived abroad with my parents for a while, which was in this place called Phnom Penh. I was not really all that comfortable with my surroundings yet, and I'd heard horror stories from my parents about how other Japanese students had this tendency to keep their distance from returnees.

Luckily, I also have a sister—who isn't actually related to me—who's spent her entire life in Japan. She said, "Sadly, that's true. They're all pathetic losers, afraid of anyone who does something different or thinks about crap in a different way. You'd better be ready."

So I was prepared for it, and just kept quiet.

Even when I didn't feel like it, I always tried to help people, and I was careful to always maintain an easy-going attitude. And somehow, I ended up getting really popular with all of the girls in class. If the girls had something they didn't understand, or something in the study guide that didn't make sense, they'd always come to me for help instead of the teacher.

"Oh, Masaki's so smart! Must be all that studying abroad."

I hadn't really studied abroad in the traditional sense of the term, but for some reason, the idea stuck.

Honestly, I was a bit out of my league. I couldn't push the girls away, but the guys in my class—in my entire school—all started to look at me funny.

By this point, high school entrance exams were right on top of us, so I wasn't exactly bullied by anyone (not much, anyway), but when I left school grounds, things would get a little…argumentative. In school, lowerclassmen would never bug an upperclassman, but once school was over, that line just vanished. I got glares from all directions.

It wouldn't have been so bad if I didn't always have a group of girls crowding around me. All they ever did was just squeal and treat me like their own little toy; never like a true friend. I was pretty fed up with it by then, but I stuck with it.

Then one day, I slipped up. Guess I must've been tired or something.

I had to swing by the station, so I cut through a back alley, and found myself surrounded by five guys.

"So, Mr. Study Abroad. You've been doing pretty well for yourself, haven't ya?"

"Getting a little bit too much attention, see?"

You'd think these guys would be dressed all trashy, but they weren't. No, they were all wearing pretty expensive jackets and didn't look like delinquents at all. So I hadn't realized what they were up to until it was too late and I was already surrounded. And by then, they already had switchblades open.

I wasn't sure how old they were, but they had to have been younger than me. One of the kids' voices had barely even cracked.

Still, that didn't make the others any less menacing.

"Right…I'll be more careful."

I'd blown it. I'd been so careful not to let myself get into a situation like this that I had walked right smack dab into one…and now they had me.

"You'll be careful? How are you gonna do *that*?"

"I'll try not to get as much attention?"

They all cackled.

Then suddenly, one shouted, "Don't you fuck with us!" And a hard punch connected with my cheek.

I saw his fist coming for me easily enough, but I let him hit me. I swung my body back a little and softened the blow.

The punch had connected enough to cut the inside of my cheek. There was blood in my mouth…but my teeth were fine. He hadn't hit any key points, so I wasn't even shaken.

This guy was nothing much. In Phnom Penh, I'd been studying a sort of undisciplined form of karate—kind of a child's self defense class, if you will—for a pretty long time. I'd learned to size up my opponents just by looking at them. Their shoulders alone were a good indicator of just how much damage a person could really do.

The most effective technique in this self-defense class was to yell for help as loud as you can. I considered this, briefly. If these were professional kidnappers, it might work, but this was Japan, and I felt that with opponents as inexperienced as these guys it would just provoke them. Plus, people tend to ignore cries for help anyway. The only real way to get anyone's attention is to just lie and scream, "Fire!"

What really had me worried was that these guys probably went to the same school as me. If I kicked their asses, they'd just come back in larger numbers, and then the trouble would never let up.

And just as I was trying to figure out if hitting them four or five times would settle things or not...

"Hey," someone said.

She was talking to all of us at once. Both the attackers and little ol' me—the victim.

"That looks boring."

Surprised, we turned and found a girl just standing there.

The first thing I noticed was her unruly hair, which seemed to have been just left there at a sort of arbitrary length. It seemed to flow out of her.

We were in a dirty back alley that stank of piss and ditch water. The sky was dark and cloudy, and I was hunched down like a sad frightened rabbit.

No matter how you looked at it, my first meeting with Orihata Aya was...anything but perfect.

***

"............"

I gaped at her for what seemed like an eternity.

The girl with her arbitrary hair never even glanced at me. She just walked briskly towards us.

"Wh-who are you? Study Abroad's girlfriend?" one snarled.

She didn't even blink. "What is your purpose? What failing of his caused this behavior?" Her voice was flat, devoid of emotion.

"Hunh? You don't know this guy?"

"What do you think you're doing here?" asked another classmate.

"I asked for a reason," she insisted.

"Hey, this guy thinks he's Don Juan. Looking like this, tricking girls into falling for him."

Obviously lies, but I fought back the anger.

"Hunh…" she said, and at last looked at me.

For some reason, I found myself glaring back at her.

She frowned. She looked at me like I puzzled her.

I thought she was pitying me, which made me angrier. I could tell my expression was growing harsher as I fought against my feelings.

She frowned harder, put her head to one side, then sort of drooped before looking back at the group around me.

"So, he stole your girlfriends, then? The cause of your anger is sexual frustration?"

She didn't even bat an eye at what she was saying.

It was so out there that we all just sort of stared.

"Uh…what? What did she say?"

"I'm asking if this attack is a way of forgetting that your sexual partners all hate you."

Her tone was so level, it couldn't be taken as deliberate provocation. She was just throwing the words out there.

They stood silently for a moment, but then their faces turned red, their fists shook. They were getting angry.

"You…bitch!" They all went for her, reaching out to grab her. And she did something none of us could have predicted.

She grabbed her own shirt, and tore it off.

Her bare chest hit the chilly night air.

It was pale and beautiful, as if it was drinking in all the light that shone around it.

"If you have frustrated desires, I can fulfill them," she said, still completely calm. The thing is, there was much more expression on her face just moments before when she had looked at me. At this moment, it was like she was wearing a mask.

"Uuuum…"

"H-hey…"

The boys froze in mid-lunge, bug-eyed.

"Whoa, wait a minute—!" I said, flustered. I didn't know what the hell was going on, but I was not about to stand by and let them do as they pleased with her.

But at that moment, a loud voice came from the far end of the alley.

"Well, *this* is easy to figure out!"

We spun around, and there was a young man in white clothes standing there.

He strode towards us confidently.

"—! Wh-who are you?!"

"Just to make sure, I'd better ask. You there," he pointed at me. "Do you want to save this girl?"

I quickly nodded, "Y-yes."

"Then take her and run!" he snapped, strode right over to her, and took the bare-chested girl by the arm.

"Hey!" one of the boys said, and moved towards him, but with blinding speed he reached out to the boy's chest…and that alone sent him flying.

Even I couldn't see what he'd done. This guy was something else.

While I was still stunned, he shoved the girl towards me.

"Go! Get out of here!!"

I managed to say, "Th-thank you," as I took the girl's arm and ran. She followed, unresisting.

When we were almost on the main street, I quickly shrugged off my jacket and covered her body with it.

"Are you okay?" I asked.

She seemed a little out of it. She stared back at me, and asked, "Why?"

"Eh?"

"Didn't you hate me?" She looked puzzled again.

I didn't get it, but I couldn't leave that man to handle those boys all by himself, so I put her on a bench in front of the station, which seemed safe enough, told her to wait for me, and hurried back.

But halfway there a hand grabbed me from behind.

I turned around, and it was the young man.

"Hey," he said, smiling. There was not a scratch on him. No dirt…not even so much as a wrinkle on his crisp white suit. Who was this guy?!

"Are…you okay?!"

"Yeah, it's all taken care of. I doubt they'll bother you again," he said airily.

I gaped at him. I'd been gone less than two or three minutes. And there'd been five of them.

"Um, y-you…"

"I think you ought to worry more about her than me. How's she doing?"

"Um, I don't…"

"Better hurry back. The girl's much less secure than she looks. Her roots and stem have merged, and you can't tell them apart. Plus, she's got very few leaves and just a hardened bud in place of a flower."

He'd lost me completely. All I could manage was a dumb-founded, "What?"

"It's not important. If she says horrible things to you, I wouldn't pay too much attention. That's the trick for getting along with her. Bye." Leaving this further cryptic comment behind him, the man in white turned and walked away.

"…………"

I stood there stunned for a moment, but soon collected myself, and hurried back to the girl.

She was sitting in exactly the same position as I'd left her, with both hands on the front of the jacket, holding it closed.

"—Um, are you feeling better?" I asked rather stupidly, unable to think of anything else.

"…………" She didn't answer.

I didn't know what to do, but now that I thought about it, she had effectively rescued me, so I said, "Uh, th-thanks. For, uh…for back there."

"Why?" she asked, looking up at me. She looked puzzled again.

Man, I couldn't get this conversation rolling at all.

"Well, you saved me, didn't you?" I said, smiling hopefully.

Her eyes widened, then for some reason she looked down, and mumbled, "…I thought you hated me."

"Hunh?" I gaped back at her. "Why? Why would I hate you?"

"I can't be hated by anyone. Not by any normal humans," she said oddly intense. Her eyes were serious.

"…I don't hate you."

"But you glared at me…" she said, very sadly.

"I did? Oh…but that wasn't about you. I just was angry with myself, so…I…I mean…" I stumbled, trying to clear things up.

Still looking at the ground, she whispered, "I'm sorry."

"Why are you apologizing? It's all my fault! *I* was worried that you hated *me*!"

She looked up. "—Why?"

"I mean, that was pretty pathetic back there, right? That's why I was angry at myself. Nothing to do with you. I was so angry because I was sure you hated me." The more I babbled, the more pathetic I came across.

She quietly watched me flail about, but said nothing.

"And then because I couldn't make up my mind, you…" I trailed off, shoulders slumping. "But it's over now. I'll pay for your clothes. Um…"

I reached for my wallet, and remembered that the reason I'd been heading for the station in the first place was that I had no money and needed to swing by an ATM.

"Ugh, crap…the ATM's already closed…!"

"Don't worry about money. I have some," she answered as she stood up.

"But I can't just do nothing…"

"Really. If you could lend me this jacket…I'll give it back."

"Oh, no—take it! But that doesn't really pay you back at all…could you at least give me your address? Or phone number? I'll call you later and I'll pay you for the clothes then…"

"………" She stared at me levelly. I was taller than her, so she had to look up at me slightly. It could be taken as a glare.

"Ah, no, I don't mean it like that. Uh…if you'd prefer to call me…yeah, we should do it that way."

"Orihata."

"Mm?"

"My name. Orihata Aya. You are…?"

"Oh, uh, I'm Taniguchi Masaki."

"Masaki…that's a nice name," and at last she smiled. A very small smile, the corners of her mouth turning up ever so slightly, but there was enough power in it to grab me by the heart.

Was this what they called love at first sight?

***

"I...I got tickets to a movie that's supposed to be really good. You...you wanna come?" I asked, finally working up the nerve to ask out Orihata. It was over the phone, but you have to go with what you have.

"Are you sure? With me?" The voice on the other end of the line said, faintly.

Hiding my tension, I replied cheerily, "I still haven't thanked you for last time. If you've got other plans, I...I understand, but..."

"...Thank you. Okay."

"You'll...you'll come?! Awesome!!!"

"But Masaki, I'm really..."

"Mm? What?"

"No...never mind." And she fell silent.

Further details were basically all decided by me, and she simply agreed to everything I suggested. I couldn't think of any clever way to say good-bye, so ended up sort of hanging up awkwardly.

I heard someone giggle behind me. At some point, my sister had come downstairs. My parents were still living abroad, so the two of us were alone in the house.

"And here I thought you were a playboy. Awfully stressed for a *simple* date, aren't we?"

"It's not nice to eavesdrop."

"I couldn't *not* hear you. Your voice was so loud, I heard it upstairs. I thought something had happened."

Considering that she spent basically all her time poking at computers in her room, she was awfully nosy at times like this.

"None of your business, Nagi! Leave me alone."

"Okay, okay. I'm not *that* bored," she said, playing dumb.

***

And on the day of our date, we got to the movie theater and realized we had underestimated the situation a bit. There was a huge crowd with the line snaking all around the theater and back out onto the street.

"The end of the line starts here," shouted a theater employee at the end of the line. "Please be advised that there is a four-hour wait!"

"Oh, wow…what should we do?" I clutched my head. I'd blown our first date. "Should we try some other day?" I asked.

Orihata looked puzzled. "Why?" she asked.

"We'll have to wait a really long time. It'll blow our whole day."

"You don't want to wait?"

"Well…doesn't it make you tired?"

"Then I'll wait in line. You go play somewhere," she said calmly, and took her place at the end of the line.

I was a mess. "What?! I can't do that! I should be the one who waits!"

"I don't mind. I'm used to doing nothing."

"No, I mean…this is supposed to be me…thanking *you*." Even as I spoke, several people got in line behind her.

"Right!" I made up my mind. I turned and ran back towards the station.

The road was filled with people. I looked around me as I ran.

"Oh, Study Abroad. What are *you* doing here?" someone asked. I spun around. It was one of the guys from my class, Anou.

"Ah, um, you know."

"Yeah, I do. You're making some chick wait for you, huh?"

The boys in my school didn't like me in the first place, but this Anou guy was one of the most aggressive. Usually, I could handle him okay, but I had no time for it today.

"Sorry, in kind of a hurry," I said, brushing him off, and dove into a fast food joint. I bought an assortment of food and drinks, and hurried back.

"Excuse me! Excuse me! Coming through…" I wormed my way through the line, earning the hatred of every single person I passed, and finally caught up with Orihata. "Sorry to keep you waiting, heh heh…"

"I thought you weren't coming back."

"We need an endurance strategy for this. Thought we ought to at least have lunch." I showed her the bag.

"But you didn't like waiting."

"Not really. But if…" I'm with you, I've got no time to be bored…I started to say, but got embarrassed, and fell silent.

"What?" Orihata asked, head to one side.

"…So, uh, what'll you have? I brought a bunch so you could choose…what do you like?"

"Anything."

"You like everything?"

"I have no right to dislike anything."

There she went again with the cryptic stuff. I couldn't get her to explain this. It was like her heart was locked down somewhere, and I couldn't get in.

So I grabbed a double cheeseburger at random and handed it to her, and began scarfing down a hot dog myself.

She began nibbling at the burger, neither reluctantly nor happily. I felt like I was feeding a rabbit, which made me uncomfortable.

I finished my hot dog in three bites, and had nothing left to do. My eyes wandered upwards towards the sky.

Suddenly, Orihata looked at my face, and exclaimed, "Ah!" Before I even had time to wonder why, she reached up, her face came close to mine, and she licked the ketchup off the side of my mouth…with her tongue!

I was stunned. She looked like nothing at all had happened.

"Now you're clean."

She wasn't at all embarrassed, and she wasn't joking around either. It was as if she had decided her tongue would be the most effective tool, since her hands were busy holding the burger. Her job complete, she turned her attention back to eating again.

Meanwhile, I had turned bright, bright red.

I'm not sure how many hours we waited, but at some point

we finally managed to make it into the theater. And before I knew it, the movie was over. I couldn't tell you a single thing that happened—I spent the entire time in a complete daze.

When I snapped out of it, we were outside, and it was already night.

All it took was Orihata telling me, "Bye," outside the theater to bring my attention crashing back to reality.

"Eh? Going home already?" I'm sure I sounded a little whiney.

Orihata looked a little surprised. "But…we already saw the movie."

"Yeah, but…we could go to a cafe or something," I said, wistfully.

"Really?"

"Of course! It'll be on me!"

"Not the money…you don't think I'm boring?"

"No, not at all!" I said, flustered. I thought she must be angry with me, since I'd been so out of it.

But Orihata looked relieved, and said, "Good. I was worried. I thought you hated me."

I never in a million years thought she would say that, so I panicked a little. We somehow made it into a nearby cafe, *Tristan*, ordered some coffee, and at last, I settled down. This was the chance I needed to sort everything out, so I tried talking with her.

"Orihata, you don't think…*I'm* boring?" Oh god, that was terrible. Still, I couldn't not ask that.

But Orihata didn't answer. Instead, she suddenly took my

hand. Her gentle touch wrapped around my wrist.

I was taken aback, but I couldn't snatch my hand away, so I just sort of jumped in my seat dramatically.

"Masaki…your skin is warm," she said with a peaceful expression on her face, like an old lady who had just sipped some really good tea.

She was a mystery. I understood nothing about her.

***

And that's basically how Orihata and I started going out, although it was a strange sort of relationship, and I'm not really sure you could call it dating.

First of all, her house…

No matter when I called, she always answered instantly—right in the middle of the first ring. I had barely finished dialing, and the call was connected, and BAM! There she was saying, "Orihata," with absolutely no emotion at all.

"Um, it's Taniguchi…" No matter how many times I called, I always started out tongue-tied.

"What?" she always said, curtly.

"Um, well, I thought this Saturday…"

Our relationship was awfully like this phone call. I got all excited and chased after her, but she was completely neutral.

But even though the high school entrance exams were right in front of me, I spent all of my free time with her. In my case, I had already been successfully admitted to a private high school a year before (but one condition for my acceptance was that I graduate from a Japanese Junior High, which is why I'd moved back here), so I had nothing to worry about. Still, I was a little worried about her. I asked once, but she just shrugged.

"You haven't decided?" It was already mid-January.

"I'll be taking a test, but I don't know which school yet," she said, as if she was talking about someone else.

"Are your parents strict?"

"I don't have any."

"Hunh? What?"

"Parents."

"But that…" Apparently she had no parents, and lived alone. In high school…I could see it, but in Junior High? "No relatives at all?"

"…………" No answer.

"Sorry, I…I shouldn't have asked," I said apologetically.

She turned towards me suddenly. "Sorry, Masaki," she said, rather urgently.

"About what?" I asked, surprised.

She looked at the ground. "I'm sorry. I can't tell you," she murmured.

I couldn't ask further. It hurt me to see her sad. Whenever she did, I would get really cheery and try to slide past it. "Gosh, the sky is really beautiful today, huh?!" I might say, in a stupidly loud voice.

She almost never smiled, but when we separated, she always asked if we could meet again, so I guess she didn't hate me. At least, that's what I kept telling myself.

Eventually, I don't know how, she decided to go to high school at Shinyo Academy.

"Oh! Congratulations!" I said happily, when she told me on the phone that she had passed the test.

"I'm glad you're happy, Masaki," she replied. She almost never sounded like she was having fun, but that day…she did.

"We should do something to celebrate. What do you think? Meet in a few at the usual place?"

"Yes, okay."

Happily, I rushed out to the park where we always met. Not knowing what was waiting for me.

***

"Yes, okay. Mmhmm…mmhmm…bye."

Orihata Aya hung up her cell phone after her conversation with Taniguchi Masaki.

It had been the first time she had ever called him. Until now, she had always waited for him to call, but Masaki had been worried about what high school she was going to, so she thought she should let him know.

He had been happy. That made Aya happy. He was unaware that "higher education" was merely a camouflage for her "mission." She was not happy about it. She did not feel anything about it. But if something she did made Masaki happy, then Aya was happy too.

She moved quickly towards her closet.

Since she met Masaki, her wardrobe had increased dramatically. If she wore something nice, Masaki would tell her it was cute, so Aya began paying attention to her clothes.

There was nothing else in her room. With the exception of the furniture provided by the building's landlord, there were no other furnishings. No TV, no table, not even a bed. There was but a single sleeping bag lying on the floor.

She changed, and went out, allowing the muscles in her cheeks to relax slightly.

People hardly ever came to the park where they always met. It was a large green belt surrounded by three highways, which made it a little scary for parents to take their children out to play. Unfortunately, it was also a tad too out in the open for young people, so it was like an empty air pocket smack dab in the center of the city.

Aya sat down on a bench.

Waiting for Masaki as the rays of the afternoon sun came through the trees above her, Aya entertained the brief fantasy that she was a normal, happy girl.

She didn't know exactly what Masaki thought of her. But when she thought of the secrets she was keeping from him...no matter what he wanted from her, he would still be important to her.

If he knew the truth, would he still be her friend? This was her greatest fear.

With her head down, Aya waited for Masaki, not moving.

She was always worried that he wouldn't come. But she

couldn't possibly arrive after him. It would be awful if he hated her because of that. So she always came an hour before they were supposed to meet. But today was quite sudden, so she only had to wait another ten minutes or so.

As Aya glanced at her watch, a shadow stood before her.

She thought it was Masaki, and looked up, blushing slightly. Her expression froze.

"_____!"

It wasn't him. It was a very fat man, with graying hair and a broad grin. Big, round, glittering eyes.

"What are you doing, 'Camille'?" the man said to Aya, in a high, reedy voice. The black leather jacket he wore was open at the front, but looked ready to burst apart at the seams at any moment. It shone with a tasteless gleam. There was a belt round his waist with a number of pockets hanging from it, each of which had a cell phone in it.

"Nothing of any purpose," Aya replied, dutifully answering to the name 'Camille,' eyes down towards the ground.

"Meeting a boy? Remember who you are," the fat man sneered. When he laughed, his eyes didn't budge, but stayed perfectly round.

His fat lay entirely on his head and belly, which were perfectly round, but his arms and legs were thin and long like poles. He looked very unhealthy. He had almost no neck. Strongly defined features and swollen cheeks, like he'd placed pads on the sides of his face.

At that moment, a gust of wind swept by, lifting his long,

greying hair. His right ear was missing. There was only a jagged wound, like it had been torn off.

The man straightened his hair, hiding the injury.

"........." Aya's head was still down.

"Look up," the man said, and she obeyed, moving jerkily.

He glared down at her frostily. "Have you done him?"

"...No, not yet."

"What are you waiting for? Let him have you. You're in no position to make a big deal out of something like that."

"Yes......"

"Well, not like *that mission* has to be in any hurry...but the other one does. Have you found any clues?"

"No, I—" Aya started to say, but was abruptly cut off as the man punched her in the face.

Aya fell off the bench, and sprawled on the pavement. Her lip was split and bleeding.

"............"

But her expression registered neither pain nor anger.

"You just don't get it, Camille, do you? What are you? *Mm?* You don't perform your duty. You're nothing but a defective product."

He slowly waddled over to her, and kicked her in the side. He kicked her again and again, and each time her body shook.

"............"

But still her expression didn't change.

"You see? I'm not letting you stay alive out of pity. If you aren't useful to the Towa Organization...if you aren't useful to me…I'll dispose of you whenever I wish. We've got a lot more where you came from!"

He grabbed Aya's collar, and yanked her upwards, putting his face right in hers.

"Now you listen to me. He's in this area." His voice went low and quiet, like a knife twisting in her gut. "I don't know why, but all the young girls in this area know about him. It's idle gossip, but they know of him. There must be something. Finding out what that is…is your job. Not walking around and just wasting time with a guy you're not even having sex with. Got me?"

"I understand, Spooky E." Aya answered quietly, emotionless.

And then, someone called out, "Hey! What are you doing?!"

Spooky E twisted his head towards the voice. It was Taniguchi Masaki.

"Let go of her!" he screamed, running towards them.

"……! N-no!" Aya cried, terrified.

"Mm?" Spooky E frowned at her emotion, but quickly grinned, and dropped her. "You must be lover boy."

He turned towards Masaki, on his guard.

"What did you do to her?!" Masaki yelled, furious, and uncharacteristically came right at Spooky E, swinging his fist.

"No, Masaki! Run away!" Aya screamed, desperate.

"Hunh…" Spooky E made a light step sideways, dodging the blow.

Spooky E tried to punch Masaki in the back, but Masaki had read the movement and was able to twist his body enough to dodge the blow and recover his distance.

"……!" Spooky E looked alarmed.

Masaki got his balance back, and hit a stance.

But he was far more tense than the fat man.

(…this guy was pulling back…but I still barely dodged him.)

He should never have been able to move like that at his weight. However…

Masaki's instincts told him to ignore common sense. This was clearly no ordinary opponent.

"……Mmph…" Cold sweat ran down his brow.

Spooky E spoke to the fallen Aya. "Is this guy some sort of stupid martial artist? Or is he an MPLS? Is he an enemy of the Towa Organization?!"

"——!" Aya's face turned white. "Nothing like that! Masaki's a normal human!" she almost shrieked, like Masaki's life depended on her answer.

"Ah, so he's just some average Joe that thought he'd learn a little kung fu."

"……?" Masaki glanced at Aya. These two knew each other? Aya avoided his eyes.

Spooky E took advantage of this drop in his guard, and lunged at him.

Too fast for the eye to follow, he closed the gap between them.

"Wah!" Instincts screaming danger as Masaki made no attempt to guard. He simply fled the attack.

He rolled on the ground.

But this took him farther away from Aya.

"——! Oh no!" He wasn't thinking clearly.

He tried to get near her quickly, but Spooky E was right there in his way.

"You can't leave her and run away alone, eh? What a hero."

"…………"

"If you were an MPLS, I might have to be careful…but an ordinary human? Let me show you why they call me…Spooky Electric." He opened his fists.

On his palms, his blood vessels stood out unnaturally. Blue and red lines ran all across them.

Masaki thought he could hear a crackle coming from them…

"O-Orihata! Run!" he yelled, sensing danger.

But Aya just slumped, making no attempt to stand.

"Shit…!" Masaki rushed forward, desperately.

Grinning, Spooky E waited for him.

Inside, Masaki thought, 'To hell with it,' and, grinding his teeth, he aimed a kick right at Spooky E's unguarded crotch.

His karate master had told him, "If you really need to, don't hesitate."

Masaki's toes struck directly at every man's weakest point.

But…the sensation was all wrong.

"—Hunh?!" He looked up at his enemy's face.

The grin was still there, the same as ever.

"Too *baaaad*," he said, and with a quick little jitterbug of a step, Spooky E put his palms on Masaki's head, one on each side.

Everything went black before Masaki's eyes, and he passed out.

***

My head throbbed.

I could hear voices, but they seemed so far away…

"Please, let him be. We haven't yet. There's still a chance…"

"He got to you pretty good, huh? But if that boy knew what you've been up to, he won't think the same…"

"I know…but please…spare him."

"Huh? You aren't even human. What are you thinking?"

"Please…"

"Okay, then. I'll let him live…on that one condition."

"Thank you."

"But don't forget, Camille. Your primary mission is to find *him*. Find that——"

That was all I heard. After that, I knew nothing more.

***

And when I woke up, it felt very warm all around me.

"Uh……?" I opened my eyes, stretching. Orihata's face was right above me.

"You woke up," she said, gently.

Surprised, I sat up, looking around. We were in the park where I had apparently fallen asleep on a bench.

On her lap no less.

"Wh-what? Why am I sleeping here?"

I shook my head, but the last thing I could remember is getting a phone call from Orihata, and suggesting we celebrate her getting accepted into high school. I couldn't remember what I did after that. I couldn't even remember arriving at the park.

"I think you got sunstroke. When I got here, you were already asleep," Orihata said calmly.

"Really? I was sleeping?"

"It surprised me. I thought you were dead…"

"Wow…I'm s-sorry. But sunstroke?" It was sunny enough, but it was barely spring. Much too early to get sunstroke, right?

"Sorry, this is all my fault…" she said.

"N-no it isn't! I'm the one who passed out!" I said hurriedly.

It seemed like I was always showing her these awkward undignified moments.

"S-so we were going to celebrate, right? Is there anything you'd like me to do? Go ahead, ask me anything," I said, cheerfully, grinning, trying desperately to cover.

She looked suddenly very sad.

She stood up from the bench, turning her back on me.

There was a long silence.

"…………"

Her figure seemed to absorb the rays of the setting sun, like she was melting into the backlight.

She looked very fragile, almost like a ghost.

After a minute of silence, I gingerly asked, "Wh-what's wrong?"

"Masaki...you're really strong, aren't you?" she whispered, not turning around.

"Um?"

"When we first met...if I hadn't saved you, you'd have been able to get out of that on your own, right?"

Suddenly, I found myself in a very awkward position. "Uh, w-well, that's not..."

"Masaki, can I ask you a favor?" Her voice came over her shoulders.

"Yes. Anything!"

"Masaki, you're friends with the girls in this area, right?"

"Uh, yeah...I-I guess."

"I wonder if you've heard anything from them...rumors of a mysterious *shinigami*."

"Rumors?"

"Nobody knows where he appears, but all the girls know his name." She turned around. The backlight hid her face, and I couldn't make out her expression. "They all know about Boogiepop."

III

Do not doubt your work.
No matter how pointless or unrewarding it
may appear to be, anything is better than
knowing for certain that is actually is.

—Kirima Seiichi (*VS Imaginator*)

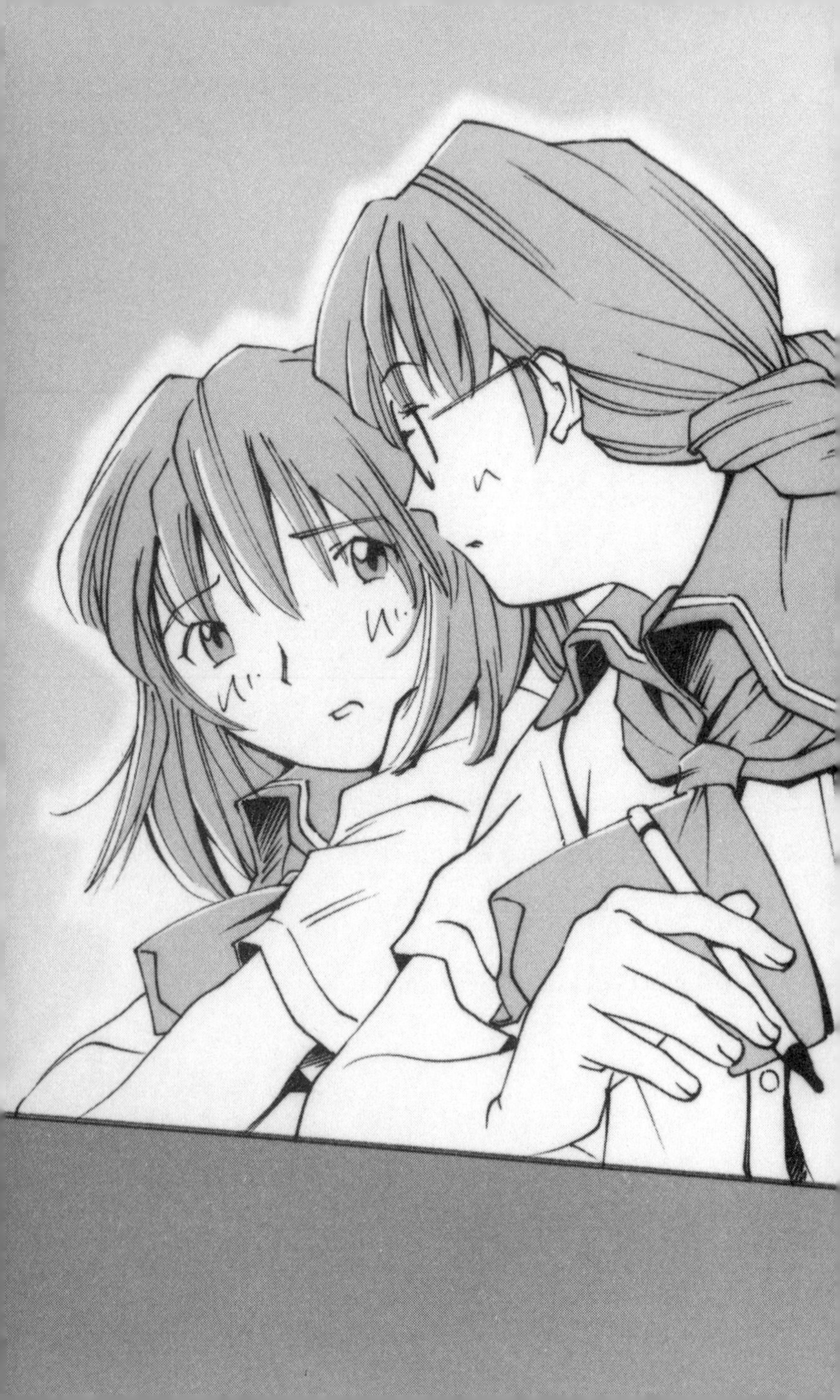

"Um, so if x is an imaginary number, then the range of y is...a complete mystery. Suemaaaa! Help meeee...!"

One day late in March, my friend Miyashita Touka and I were hunched over our study guides in a quiet corner of the freshly emptied cram school. There was nobody else around.

This year's students had mostly taken their tests and stopped coming, and next year's crowd wouldn't start attending seriously until next week. It was like a little breathing room between tests.

"We've only been studying twenty minutes. It's too soon to give up."

"Yeah...but I have. My head's already spinning from all those numbers. If I see another equation, I'm gonna hurl!"

"Not like you're a drunk or anything..." I giggled. Touka was at best artless and at worst...a little on the rude side, but still, I thought she was refreshing. At least, she always admitted it when she didn't understand something.

"Come on, help me here, Kazuko-chaaaan! How does this thing work?" With a labored expression, she glared fiercely at the study guide, poking at it with the tip of her pencil.

This year, we would finally be seniors. While we'd effectively been so since January, once April came around, we would officially make the switch from being laid-back high school students to stressed-out exam students.

I met Touka back during the winter course at this cram school, and that was where I learned that we went to the same high school, but somehow had managed to completely avoid running into each other. And even now, we pretty much only saw each other at cram school.

Still, we hit it off really well. I'm a little warped because of some stuff in my past, but she came over to me despite all that.

"Well, this one…" I leaned over, and started explaining the problem to her.

"Uh huh. Uh huh." Touka sat up, and leaned her entire upper body onto the table. From the side, we must've looked like we were about to arm wrestle. The very thought amused me.

"Got that?"

"Umm…well…kind of."

"Then explain it back to me."

"Eh heh. That…that might be pushing things," Touka replied, looking extremely embarrassed.

"Tut tut. You've got to understand this properly," I said.

Touka giggled. "I'm sorry. It's like I'm turning you into my own private tutor. And you're not even getting paid. Still, if I didn't make smart friends, I'd be totally screwed…"

"You aren't gonna sweet talk your way out of this."

"Ah, you noticed."

"Yep. So, how do we use that equation to solve this problem?"

"Um…pass!"

"You can't do that! We're not playing *shogi* here…"

Studying for exams was never easy, but at moments like this, it could be a lot of fun.

While Touka was grappling with the problem, I glanced away, turning my gaze to a painting that was hung on the wall.

It was a strange picture of a large number of people holding hands, sprawled on the ground of a wasteland. The style was pretty rough, with a lot of pencil traces left in it, and to me, it felt awfully dated for such a hip cram school.

It was an abstract oil painting. The title was "Snow Falling in April." The painter was Asukai Jin, who was one of the teachers that worked here. This painting had won some kind of an award and was probably just hung on the wall to make the school look more important than it was.

Because of certain events in my past, I got pretty interested in criminal psychology and the unconscious psyche. This fascination has led me to read all I could find on those subjects, so it was out of habit that I started analyzing the painting in-depth.

(Hmm…the sky is cloudy…it lacks width. Must be a very closed off painting. But there's something cheerful about it. Or maybe just shallow. The wasteland clearly represents a feeling of emptiness, so why is it I get a hint of deep conviction behind it?)

With all those people, why weren't any of them looking at each other?

"It's a weird painting," Touka said, following my gaze.

"Yeah…something about it I just don't *like*," I said in a snobbish 'Oh, I hate this painting' sort of way. It might be a good painting, but I just can't bring myself to like it.

"Not your type, Suema?"

"No, I think…the guy that painted this hates people like me."

Or maybe…yeah, he was the same as me. It was a natural aversion.

"That's beyond me," Touka laughed.

"Too strange?"

"Nah, it's cool. Go with your gut."

In the past, more than a few people have told me that I was strange. But Touka always accepted what I said without question. You wouldn't believe how happy that always made me feel.

"I bet he likes you, though."

"Is that a confession?" she joked, and we cackled.

A voice came from behind us, "Um, are you Suema Kazuko-san? From Shinyo Academy…?"

We turned, and there was a girl who looked about our age.

"Yes, and…you are?"

"I'm Kinukawa Kotoe. I…I go to Shinyo Academy also. I wanted to talk to you about something, Suema-san…" She opened and closed her hands. Clearly this was really important to her.

"What about?"

"Well…you know a lot, don't you? About, you know…and Kinoshita-san said you…"

"Kinoshita? You mean Kyoko?"

Kinoshita Kyoko was a former classmate of mine.

"Yes! She said Suema could keep a secret, and was very nice, and was very smart…so she said you could help me out!" Kotoe said earnestly, waving her hands around like she was worried this wasn't enough.

"Um, well…" I hadn't done that much for Kyoko, really. Just listened to her problems and told her what I thought. The person who had helped her out when she was really in trouble was another girl.

"Please, Suema-san. Help Jin-niisan!"

"H-help who? Touka, do you have…Touka?" I turned around to find Touka completely gone.

Somehow, she'd gotten up without my ever noticing, and was standing right next to this Kotoe girl.

"Sit down, Kinukawa-san," she said, and handed her a cup of coffee from the vending machine.

When the heck did she buy that?

"Th-thanks…" Kotoe bobbed her head, and took a sip of coffee from the paper cup.

"Feel better now?" Touka asked, sounding oddly masculine.

"Y-yes, thanks." Kotoe bobbed her head again.

"You need her help?" She pointed at me with her chin.

"Y-yes. And I am sorry, but, um…"

"I understand. I'm in the way. I'll leave you two alone."

"W-wait! Touka…!"

"Kinukawa-san needs your help. You should at least listen to her." She sounded like she was on stage. Touka gave me a strange, asymmetrical expression, somewhere between innocent and mocking. I got the strangest feeling that this wasn't Touka…heck, this wasn't even a girl. It was very unsettling. "Adios," she said, and was gone.

"…………"

I stared after her like I'd seen a fox.

Kotoe pressed forward, "So…"

"Mm? Oh, right…okay. If you're friends with Kyoko, then, sure, I'll hear you out," I sighed.

***

"—Asukai Jin?" I said, eyes wide. This was the first name out of Kotoe's mouth. "The painting guy?"

"Yeah. He teaches here. You know him?"

"Just the name. They say he's a pretty good counselor."

I'd heard the rumors. You went to him for guidance counseling, he'd give you very specific advice. Neither Touka nor I had ever met with the guy. A fine arts course teacher didn't really have much contact with those of us in the national science course.

"I've…heard that too. I don't really know much."

"And you are his…niece? Or cousin?" I wasn't sure which. The gist of her introduction had escaped me.

"Our parents didn't really…get along. So Jin-niisan and I

haven't been friendly for all that long, but…the first time we ever really spoke to each other was at his father's funeral. But I knew pretty much instantly that he was this really amazing guy."

"Huh…" Her story just wasn't coming together. I had to try to make sense of it somehow. "So, why does he need help?"

"Suema-san, you know a lot, right? If somebody…changes… then, I dunno…it's, like, you know, that sort of thing."

"That sort of thing?" I asked, perplexed. I found myself looking at the painting again.

There were a number of goats among the crowd. They were munching on the rose bushes that grew out of the wasteland. Black goats.

From what I know, roses are sturdy enough, and they could pretty much bloom anywhere. Though, the quality of the flowers would probably suffer. So, seeing thorny rose bushes wasn't all that surprising. But the black goats…those were usually an allegory for the devil.

They were eating the roses—flowers, leaves, thorns and all.

The picture itself didn't give off all that unpleasant of a feeling…it was pastoral and peaceful. But something about it bugged me…

"Has he suddenly become stand-offish?"

"Not that…it's like he doesn't worry anymore."

"He used to?"

"Yeah, all the time," she said forcefully. "Maybe I shouldn't be telling you this but…his father, which was like his only family…he died in kind of a strange way…"

"How?"

"Well…"

"If you don't want to talk about it, that's fine. Lately, I've been trying to avoid those kinds of stories anyway," I said, honestly.

Kotoe looked relieved. "I knew I could count on you. You seem so with it."

"Never mind that. Why do you think he's stopped worrying?" I never did like getting compliments. Especially about this type of subject. It felt like those times when somebody would tell you how cute you used to be when you were a child. It's irritating because these people are all so lost in the past.

"Mm…" Kotoe told me that Asukai Jin had been staying out all night recently. It seemed like she was monitoring his behavior pretty closely.

"And when he does come home in the morning, he just claims to have spent the night at a friend's house? No other details at all? I mean, uh, couldn't that just be what young guys do?"

"It doesn't seem like he's got a girlfriend! When he comes home, there's always….stains on his clothes. Dark red stains. They might be…"

I gulped a little at this one. "You mean, blood?"

"But he's never injured! And his clothes never look torn, so…"

"He goes out every night and comes back covered in other people's blood? That sounds like, I dunno…like a vampire or something." I shivered.

"But if I talk to the police, Jin-niisan might get arrested, and my father's always looking for an excuse to just kick him out.

Please, Suema-san, I…I don't know what to do anymore!" Kotoe buried her face in her hands.

This was starting to sound a little dangerous. I get this feeling sometimes. Like a pounding in my chest, like an itch racing all over my body.

'Come on, Kazuko! You're an exam student! You don't have time to go poking your head where it doesn't belong!' I told myself.

But…once before, I was almost killed by something I'd never seen, and I didn't find out about it until it was all over. It's because of that experience that I have this weird compulsion of mine.

A compulsion to face off against darkness.

"Um, Kinukawa-san, why don't you just leave everything up to me, okay?" I'd said, before I could stop myself.

***

And so I found myself alone just outside the cram school's guidance counseling office, which was essentially Asukai Jin's personal domain. I'd sent Kotoe home minutes before. I knew that if she'd tagged along, she'd just have gotten in the way.

There was not a soul left in the building at this time of day.

I tried the door and it opened. It wasn't locked or anything.

(Pretty careless…or is there simply nothing in here worth stealing?)

I went in. I'd been a student here for three months, but this was my first time ever setting foot inside this office. It was tiny and dark.

'It's like one of those police interrogation rooms from TV,' I thought.

There was a desk next to the teacher's chair, and a computer on top of that. I almost turned it on, but thought better of it. It was probably password protected anyway.

(There must be something…a clue as to why he's changed…)

I poked around his desk. But there was nothing there but cram school pamphlets and various papers with notes scrawled on them about students' scores for different schools…nothing to do with Asukai Jin himself.

"Hmm…"

Had I underestimated the situation? Was this too simple a way of gathering information?

"Agh…!" I said, flopping down in his chair. I slouched down a bit, but my skirt started rising up, forcing me to twist my body a bit…

And then I saw it.

There was something white under the desk, crammed all the way towards the back. Like a scrap of paper crumpled into a ball.

"Mm?"

It caught my interest, so I dove down to fish it out.

I flattened it out. It was a page of sketchbook paper with a drawing of a girl penciled on it. The artist's initial guidelines were still left below the face. Clearly a failed sketch.

"…………?"

There was something creepy about it.

I felt like I'd seen it before.

Like I knew this girl.

(Who is she?)

As I sat there thinking, I heard footsteps from the hall.

(Uh-oh…!)

I panicked. There were no other rooms in this hallway, and the only reason anyone would come down here was to come directly to this very counseling office.

(What should I do? Um…um…)

In hindsight, I should have just left the room casually. After all, the door wasn't locked, and I was a student here, so it wouldn't be at all strange if I had just simply come by for some counseling. I could always say I'd gone, but nobody was there.

But since I was feeling a little guilty, I just stayed and hid under the desk. It was a fairly large desk—it filled about a sixth of the room—with enough room for a large computer with plenty of desk space left for paperwork.

I hunched down in the shadow of the drawer, and breathed as quietly as I could. I was completely hidden.

The footsteps stopped in front of the door, and several people came in.

"—But Asukai-sensei, we really are friends. We don't hate each other at all, right, Yuriko?"

"Y-yeah…"

Sounded like two girls and a man. The man must be Asukai Jin.

"Mm, maybe a bad choice of words. See, almost all humans hate each other. I just meant that you were no exception. I'm not making it out like you two are a special case or anything."

Asukai Jin's voice was very calm, a clear, beautiful tenor.

"But, that's so…"

"………"

One of the girls was pretty outgoing, while the other one mostly did whatever she was told, it seemed.

"Shall we get started…? What is it?"

"Um…er, are we really going to…?" The stronger girl asked, sounding a little nervous.

"Everyone else is. If you don't want to join them, I'm not forcing anybody."

"No, we'll do it!" The follower said.

"Yu-Yuriko?"

"Let's do it, Misaki. I don't want to be just an exam student anymore…..!"

"Yuriko……"

"What do you think?" Asukai asked. "This is your choice to make. I can't make it for you."

"Tell me exactly what to do. That way I can…"

(What the hell are they talking about?)

Completely forgetting that I was supposed to be hiding, I started to get annoyed by the incomprehensible conversation.

Asukai continued, detached. "I can't. The Imaginator doesn't force anyone. It's a simple choice. You can influence events, or you can be swept along by them."

Imaginator?

A word I knew suddenly popped out, surprising me. That name was from the work of a writer I had been a big fan of. I wasn't sure if it had the same meaning here or not, though.

Forgetting the danger, I poked my face out a little, peering up into the room through the gap between the chair and the drawer.

The girl called Misaki was biting her fingernails.

"Asukai-sensei, can you do me alone?" Yuriko asked. The two girls had similar hair styles and faces.

"Hmm?" Asukai Jin's face was hidden from my vantage point. All I could make out were his white clothes.

He was moving slowly towards me. I stiffened, but he didn't pull the chair out. Instead, he sat down on top of the desk.

Inches from my face, he started swinging his long, slim legs. I'd never seen a man's legs this close up before. I could feel my cheeks burning, for no reason.

"Then you'd need a different partner, someone other than Kitahara-kun."

"I'll find one!"

"Wait, Yuriko!" Misaki yelped. I couldn't figure out why she was so upset.

What were they up to? What were they talking about doing?

"Like I have a choice! You don't want to?!"

"But I..."

"Get out!"

"Eh?"

"You have no right to be in the same room as Asukai-sensei!"

Yuriko yelled harshly. It was no surprise he had said that they hated each other.

"N-no! That's just…okay, I'll do it! Please, Sensei, I'll do it!" she said, turning her gaze above me, presumably looking Asukai Jin in the eye.

"All right. I respect your decision." Asukai Jin stood up.

Suddenly, he reached out his hands to the girl's chests, and started undoing the buttons, stripping their shirts right off.

(What?! Whaaaat?!!)

I panicked. I'd been worried it was something like this, but for it to be this sexual…

But the bare-chested girls turned not towards Asukai Jin, but towards each other.

They closed the gap between them, and placed their hands on each other's shoulders.

"Stop there…now, don't move," Asukai directed, just as their breasts were about to touch.

He turned his back towards me, and reached out towards their breasts.

Their transformation was dramatic.

Simultaneously, the girls flung their heads back, mouths gaping wide like some sort of animal, the air quivering at their soundless howls. The hands resting on each other's shoulders clenched up tightly, nails digging into the skin, drawing blood.

I swear this was not the kind of transformation that pain or pleasure can cause. It was like they had temporarily ceased to be human, like…like something was being torn away from them.

Asukai Jin quietly stood before them, calmly doing something I couldn't see.

Every time his shoulders shifted, the girls shook, bodies convulsing.

Like he was tinkering with them. But near as I could tell, he never touched their bodies directly. What on Earth was he doing?

"_____!!!"

The girls gave one last great spasm, and Asukai Jin moved away.

Worn out, the girls leaned against each other. They were covered in sweat.

They were panting…but their faces looked human again, reason restored.

The girls looked at each other…and giggled.

So terrifying was their expression that I felt like something had its hand around my heart.

They looked *exactly* the same.

The features of their faces had not changed. In fact, their expressions were so identical that the resemblance between them that I had noticed before had grown far *less* pronounced.

But that expression—the emotion the muscles in their faces were shifting in reaction to—I couldn't help but feel like it was identical.

"How does it feel to be true friends?" Asukai Jin asked.

"Nice…"

"Completely wonderful."

Smiling, the girls stood up, and began dressing each other.

"That's good," Asukai Jin replied, and I swear I heard a flicker of a smile in his voice.

"Asukai-sensei, we're no longer afraid of anything."

"We feel like we could change the world for you right now."

They came over to him.

They took his hands, and kissed the back of Asukai Jin's hands like a pair of princesses swearing their allegiance to some heroic knight of legend.

I was shivering so violently. It took all my self-restraint just to keep my teeth from chattering. I couldn't move for a full three minutes after they left the room.

(Wh-what was that? What just happened here......?)

Stiffly, I crawled out from under the desk, and spread out the drawing once again as my hands trembled.

I remembered her now. The girl in the sketch had gone to my high school.

Her name was Minahoshi Suiko.

But she had killed herself. She was long gone.

The sketch was clearly Asukai Jin's, though...so how in the world was he connected to her suicide?

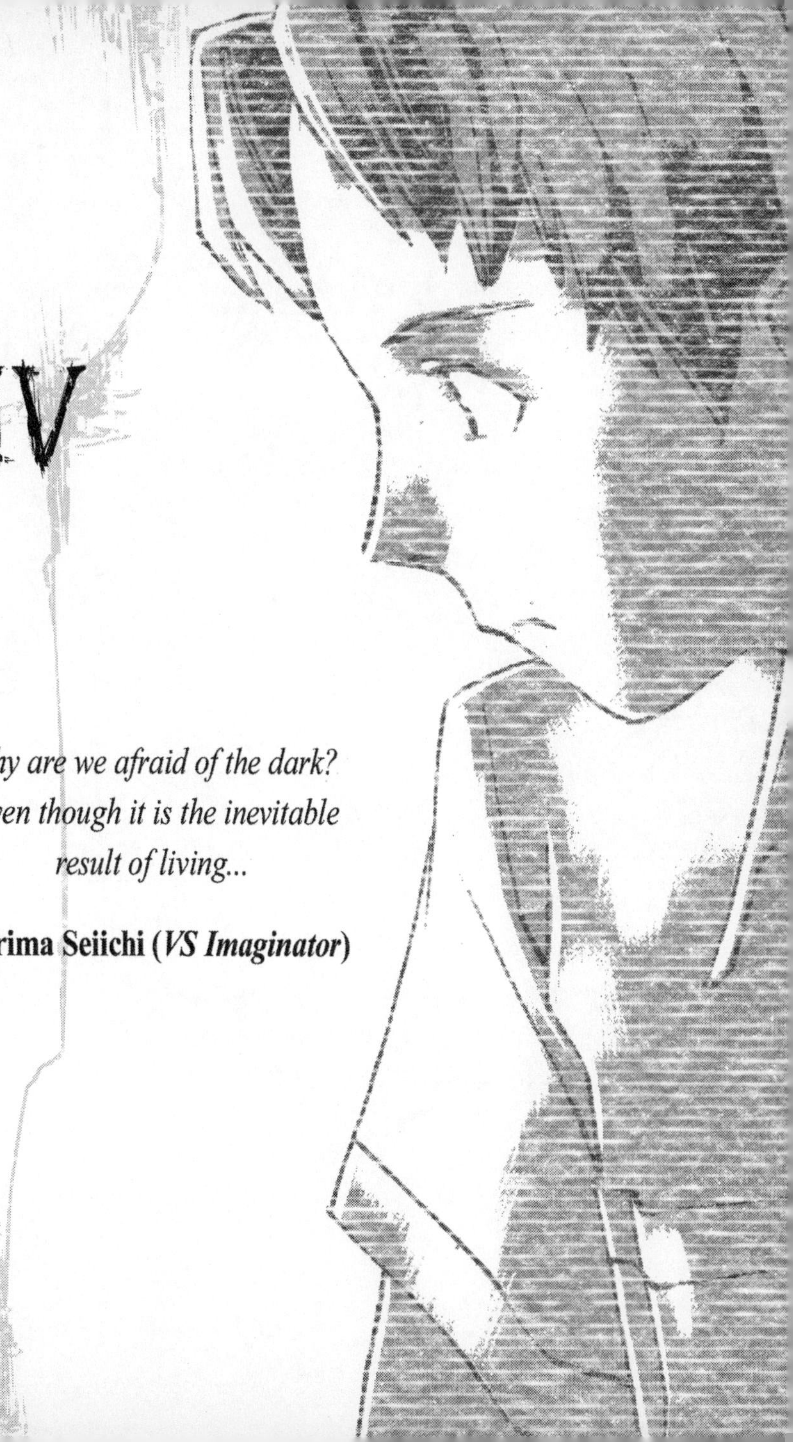

IV

Why are we afraid of the dark?
Even though it is the inevitable
result of living...

—Kirima Seiichi (*VS Imaginator*)

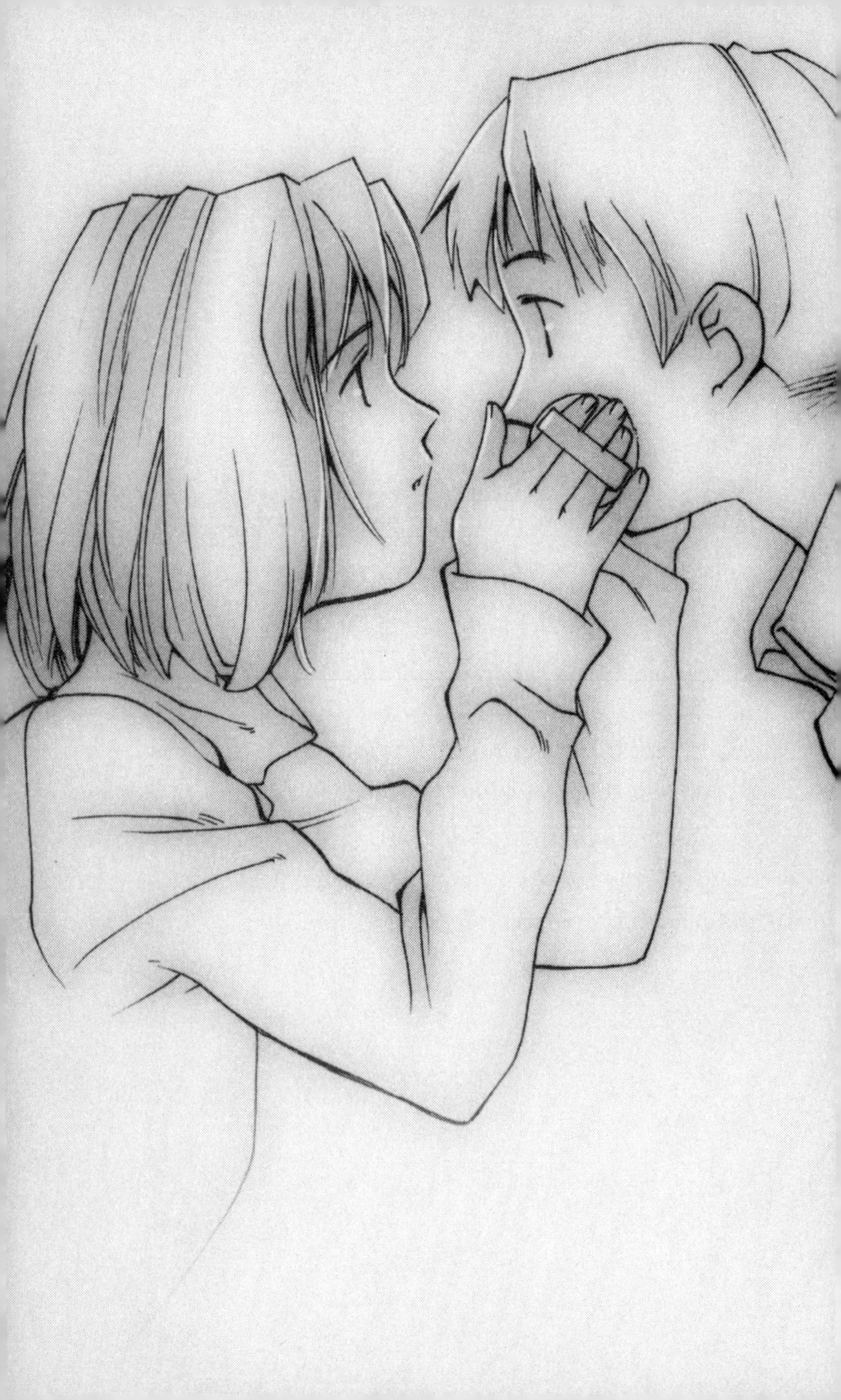

It's often said that every town has two faces, one for day and one for night. That's true enough, I suppose, but realistically, the difference is not so distinct, not so clear. Sadly, there is really no easily understood line drawn between the territory of safe, happy daylight and the sinister domain of the night.

For example, right now there's a girl sitting on a bench in front of a train station, sunlight gleaming brightly all around her. She's wearing traditional casual fashion, and anyone who looked at her would think she was a very ordinary middle class girl.

She appears to be waiting for somebody. She's got a town events guide rolled up in her hand, and she keeps tapping the ground with the toe of her shoe.

But if you watch the girl long enough, you'll begin to see a pattern hidden in the tapping. There's a rhythm to it, the same spacing between the taps, repeating.

Wait a little longer, and at last a boy comes over to her. He looks ordinary as well, clothes and hairstyle pretty bourgeois, like he gets a decent allowance.

"Yo! Waiting for someone?"

Not the most natural pick up line ever, but not likely to attract much attention if overheard.

"Yeah, at one o'clock," the girl nods. Mind you, the time is well past three.

"Okay, this way," the boy says, jerking his chin for her to follow.

This particular location has a police box in it, and there's never been a fight here. It's just that kind of place.

Whether she'd been waiting for him, or waiting for someone else, they leave the square together and head into town.

They look like any other young couple. They don't stand out at all. Why, they are the most ordinary pairing in the world.

They wander towards a deserted area of town, a zone slated for redevelopment.

The old buildings haven't been knocked down yet, and they're surrounded by dingy office buildings and crumbling stores that have long since shed all signs of what they used to sell.

The whole lot is surrounded by ropes with "no trespassing" signs hung on them. Yet the young couple pays them no attention, and ducks right under.

They turn down a narrow space between two buildings, where several men are waiting for them.

"There you are."

"Only one today?"

These 'men' all appeared to be less than twenty years old.

The boy quickly goes over to them, and they all look the girl over for a moment.

She stands and takes it. "………"

"So, how much do you want, girl?" the oldest looking of the men asks. He wears a leather jacket and flashes her a sleazy grin.

"Everything," the girl answers back, emotionless.

"Huh?"

"*I'd like you to give me everything you have*," the girl says without a trace of hesitation.

The men look a little put out. "Girl, do you even know what you're doing? You know who we are?" the guy in the leather jacket says fiercely.

"I do. You're flunkies for a drug dealer. You sell drugs to whoever gives the signal." Her face is completely calm, no eagerness, nothing unnatural.

"Flunkies?! What we got here's gonna go for a few million. You got that kinda cash?"

"No," the girl says flatly.

This outlandish declaration leaves the men gaping. "What?! What'd she say?!"

"I have no money. But like I said, I'll be taking all your drugs now." You could even call her voice chilly.

The flabbergasted men's shoulders gradually start to shake. Obviously, from anger.

"You asked for it!"

"Little bitch!"

The men launch themselves at her.

She turns and runs.

"Wait right there!"

"Don't even think about getting away!"

"I don't need to," the girl says, and turns the corner.

The first man after her rounds the corner, and the moment he does, he goes flying over backwards.

"_____!"

The men's eyes bug out of their heads.

A figure stands before them in a very strange outfit.

He's dressed in a long, black cape and wears a black hat shaped like a pipe atop his head. His face is covered in make up, white face contrasting with black lipstick. It's a hideously embarrassing outfit, completely retarded.

"Um, don't do anything stupid. You cannot defeat me," the cloaked figure stammers. It's clear why the first man went flying—this cloaked figure packs one hell of a punch.

"What the hell are you?!" The men gape. Understandably.

"I'm calling myself Boogiepop...apparently," the weirdo says, with a strange lack of confidence.

"Huh?"

"You some kinda cosplayer or somethin'?"

"Of course you've never heard of me. Only the girls know," the weirdo mutters to himself.

"What?"

"Oh, never mind."

The girl comes up behind the weirdo. And like she's reading

a script, she exclaims, "Boogiepop! These people are bad! Get them!!"

"Right, I've had just about enough of…"

The men move to attack. Several of them are clearly experienced fighters. They know what they're doing.

…So I couldn't hold back.

***

As soon as all the men had been thoroughly beaten, the cloaked figure went through their pockets, and removed a large number of little plastic bags filled with drugs.

Stuffing these into the pack on his side, the weirdo darted away.

His breathing was ragged, less from exhaustion than panic, and at last, he took shelter under a rarely used pedestrian overpass.

The girl was waiting for him there—Orihata Aya.

"Thank you, Masaki," Orihata said, smiling.

The cloaked weirdo took off his black hat.

That weirdo was me—Taniguchi Masaki.

"Ugh! This outfit is freakin' hot!" I griped. "You have no idea how hard it is to fight dressed in this thing!"

"But according to the rumors, this is the outfit he wears," Orihata said, moving around behind me and untying the cloak.

"Girls' rumors! I bet they never put any thought behind them at all. *Grr.*"

"Towel," she said, handing it over. I scrubbed my face with

it, and the make up came off soon enough. I felt much better already.

Obviously, I had been following them since Orihata left the station.

As soon as she entered the redevelopment zone, I quickly hid in the shadows and changed…even went to the trouble of putting black lipstick on to seal the effect.

What was I doing, you say?

Well…I was playing super-hero.

I was punishing all the evildoers in town. But please, don't ask me why. This was all Orihata's idea.

She took the pouch off my hip, scooped the drugs out of it, tore open each of the bags, and poured the contents out in the nearest ditch. The brown water dissolved the white powder relatively quickly, and there was no sign of it a minute later.

'Millions of yen, they said…' I thought, absently. Not that I thought it was a waste, or that I wanted that money. It's just that for most people, I could see how that amount of cash could easily become a motive for doing something illegal.

"You're a hero, Masaki," Orihata announced.

"I…I guess."

"Thanks to you, about a hundred people have been saved from drug addiction. That's a *good* thing." She sounded like she was still reading off some invisible cue cards plastered nearby. And the tone of her voice made it hard to tell if she was being serious or still playing along.

I just didn't get it. She had known all the signs and code words for that transaction earlier, but how the heck would a girl like her know that kind of crap? I asked, of course, but all she said was, "Almost everyone knows."

"Oh? Your hand…" Orihata's gaze stopped on my left hand. I had grazed it, and there was a little fresh blood on the surface.

"Just a scratch."

"I'm sorry. It's all my fault," she said, taking my hand gently, and tending to the wound with a first aid kit she'd brought with her.

Her hand was so soft, and her face was close enough that I could feel the warmth of her breath.

Beneath the deserted walkway, it was just me and a girl standing close together, bound by a shared secret. The sad thing is, I'd never even held her hand.

And before I knew it, I was a hero.

What am I *doing*…?

***

"—They all know Boogiepop," she said. It was the first time she ever used that name. "Do you?"

"Never heard of it. Uh, what is it?"

"They say he's a *shinigami*. Or a killer."

"A…?" I gaped at her.

She just continued on. "It's just an urban legend, some sort of monstrous character, but they say this boy kills people when they are at their most beautiful, before they have a chance to grow old and ugly. That sort of thing."

"Weird." It certainly sounded like the sort of thing that would show up in girls' horror stories. I bet he was supposed to be pretty also. "So what?"

"Masaki…will you *become him*?"

"Uh, ex-excuse me?"

"I know you can do it. You're so strong. You might be a little tall, but not by too much."

"W-wait a sec! This is a killer, right?" My mind reeled. I couldn't follow the first thing she said.

"No, the killer thing is nothing more than reputation. In fact, he seems to save people more often than kill them."

She was talking like this guy actually existed.

"Y-you want me to s-save people? From what?"

"Anything."

"Anything?"

"Anything we can."

"…………"

"You're strong, Masaki. You can become Boogiepop." She stared at me intently.

Overwhelmed, I fell silent.

Her gaze suddenly shifted away. "I'm sorry. I know I have no right to ask something like this of you…"

She hung her head. Her shoulders shook.

Deflated like that, she looked so small. I felt like my chest was being torn apart.

"So if I…become this Boogie-whatsit, will that…make you happy?" I asked, unable to bear the silence.

She looked up. "Will you?"

"Sure, I'll do it. I don't know what it is I'm doing, but I'll do what I can."

"Really…?"

"Yeah," I replied, too embarrassed to add, 'If it makes you happy.'

"I'm sorry, Masaki," she buried her face in her hands. "I really am. This is too much to ask…"

"I said it was okay. We're friends, aren't we?"

"I'm so sorry…"

She always seemed so sad. She apologized so often that I felt I had to do something. Still, I couldn't shake the feeling that I'd taken a step into some strange new dimension.

***

At that time, I was unfortunately still unaware that Boogiepop wore such an embarrassing outfit.

Orihata bought a huge swath of black cloth, almost like a theater curtain, at a do-it-yourself fabric shop, and fashioned a cloak and hat out of it. I was appalled when she showed it to me. It was hideous.

"You want me to walk outside…in *this*?"

"You will change before you 'appear.' Until then, it can remain hidden…in a sports bag or something."

She produced a big Nike bag from out of seemingly nowhere.

"W-wait, I…I really have to put this stuff on?"

This was like what a street performer would wear from some long forgotten decade.

Despite my concerns, Orihata simply said, "That's how it goes."

I took the cloak, the decorations clattering, thinking again that this was a step I shouldn't be taking.

It was well made. She'd sewn it carefully, and the fabric was doubled over. It was really thick. You would never think for a minute that it was handmade, which made it all the more serious…and more embarrassing to boot.

"But what if someone I know sees me?" I asked, still underestimating my predicament.

Orihata answered that one easily. "Don't worry. You'll be wearing make-up. No one will ever recognize you."

***

This all brings us back to the here and now, with Boogiepop roaming the streets.

The first thing we tried was to have Orihata walk down backroads at night and try to attract would-be molesters, which I would then proceed to beat the ever-loving crap out of. As heroic as it sounds, I felt like I was working some sort of con. Still, if someone tried to attack Orihata, I wasn't about to just stand there and let them have their way with her.

"I thought you could do it. You're really strong," she said.

I am a guy, after all, so I can't say that hearing that didn't make me happy.

So, we kept it up, like today.

Until I started doing this, I really had now idea how danger-ous this town really is. Don't believe what people tell you. Japan isn't nearly as safe a place as the government and media leads you to believe. The proof was in how easy it was for Orihata—our "bait"—to lure in prey.

If you must know, my karate master had been forced to leave Japan after an epic bout of violence, but a man with as powerful a sense of justice as he had could hardly have lived in Japan without getting mixed up in stuff. I was no different than my master at this very moment. Which is why if he only knew his student was following in his footsteps…he'd be furious!

But why exactly Orihata wanted me to do this; that was something that I couldn't for the life of me figure out. The most worrisome thing of all was the more that I did it, the more I found myself enjoying this little "game." And not just because I was with Orihata…

"School's going to start up again pretty soon. What then?" I asked, as I stood there in a back alley, letting her apply my Boo-giepop make-up.

"…………." She didn't answer.

After covering my face with skin cream, she began patting white foundation all over it.

"Be honest, how long can we really keep this up?"

"…………." She said nothing, calmly applying my eyeliner.

Her face was inches from mine. Her lips were slightly puckered, as if she were about to kiss me.

"What do you say?"

"…………"

Boogiepop's face was apparently very, very pale. Below the eyes there were black lines, or blueish shadows. Then on top of that, he wore a hat that covers his eyes, making him look inhuman—like a ghost. If I met him on some darkened street at night, I'd probably wet myself.

"Well?" I kept asking.

She looked away, and then I heard her say, "Masaki…"

"Yes?"

"Is there anything you want me to do?"

"That came out of the blue…"

"I'll do anything. Ask me anything at all. Anything you want to do, Masaki…we'll do it." She never looked at me, but the words burst out of her.

I was stunned.

"I know it won't be enough. But if there's anything I can do…I'll do it…anything and everything you desire, Masaki. I'll do everything you want from me…"

I'd never seen her so desperate.

Her profile trembled. She seemed so wretched. I felt a pain in my chest, like it was on fire. I felt a surge of misdirected emotions.

"In that case, I'll play Boogiepop as good as I can," I said, shoulders slumping.

Her head snapped up, and she stared at me. It was her usual response, "Why?"

"Well…to tell you the truth, it's getting kinda fun." It wasn't a lie. I'd only recently come to that very revelation myself.

"Masaki…" Her hands reached towards me…then stopped, flailed around in the air a bit, and dropped limply to her sides. "You're an idiot, Masaki," she whispered.

"I know," I grimaced.

Call it irresponsible, but whatever happens, happens.

***

That day, they caught nothing. Aya went to dangerous spot after dangerous spot, but nobody came after her.

"I'm a little relieved," Masaki said. "If you got attacked every time, that'd be pretty crazy. Not to mention, scary." He took off his outfit, and handed it to Aya, like always. It was her job to look after the outfit. She would patch up any rips or tears, but today there weren't any.

"Masaki, how do you…" Aya started to ask, standing on the darkened night street.

But Masaki was busy wiping the make-up off his face, and didn't hear her.

"Uh, what'd you say?" he asked, rubbing cleansing cream over his skin.

"Nothing," Aya said, letting the question remain unspoken. She had almost asked, 'How do you feel about me?' But no matter what the answer might've been, Aya could do nothing about it…because she was lying to him.

"I'll take you home then."

"No need."

"Don't be silly. After all the times you've been attacked, I'm not letting you go anywhere without me," Masaki smiled. They had this exchange every time.

They went to the bus terminal near the station, got on a late night bus, and headed towards her apartment.

They said nothing as they rode.

Aya couldn't figure out what to talk about, and Masaki felt no need to talk. Aya glanced over at him from time to time, and every time his eyes were always there looking at her with a smile on his face. It was as if just being with her was fun enough.

Whenever Aya saw that carefree grin, her chest hurt.

She didn't know what to do.

"I'm sorry…" she whispered, inaudible above the noise of the bus.

He leaned in, "What?"

"Nothing," she said, shaking her head.

At length, the bus reached their stop.

They got off, and Masaki walked her all the way to the elevator door.

But that was all. He followed her no further.

"Night."

"Good night." Aya could think of nothing else to say.

With the Nike bag containing the Boogiepop outfit slung over her shoulder, the elevator doors closed, and headed upwards.

She bit her lip.

Something moved inside her jacket. Her phone was ringing. She jumped, and answered, "Orihata."

"Camille?" This voice was always hostile.

"Y-yes."

"You still haven't caught him?"

"At…at this point, there has been no contact," Aya's voice trembled slightly.

"Hmph. I thought a fake was too cheap a gambit for him…so we need to put a bullet in this plan."

"Which means…?" Aya felt her backbone turn to ice.

The malevolent voice continued, "We've got a different use for Taniguchi Masaki. Time for you to cut him loose."

"……!"

"Soon enough, we'll need to sterilize the area. I'll have further instructions for you. Until then, keep things going." He hung up.

"………!" Aya stood frozen in horror.

The elevator stopped, and the doors opened, but her legs were shaking so much that she was frozen in place. Seconds later, the doors closed again in front of her.

V

It is easy to become carefree.
All you have to do is lose your soul.

—Kirima Seiichi (*VS Imaginator*)

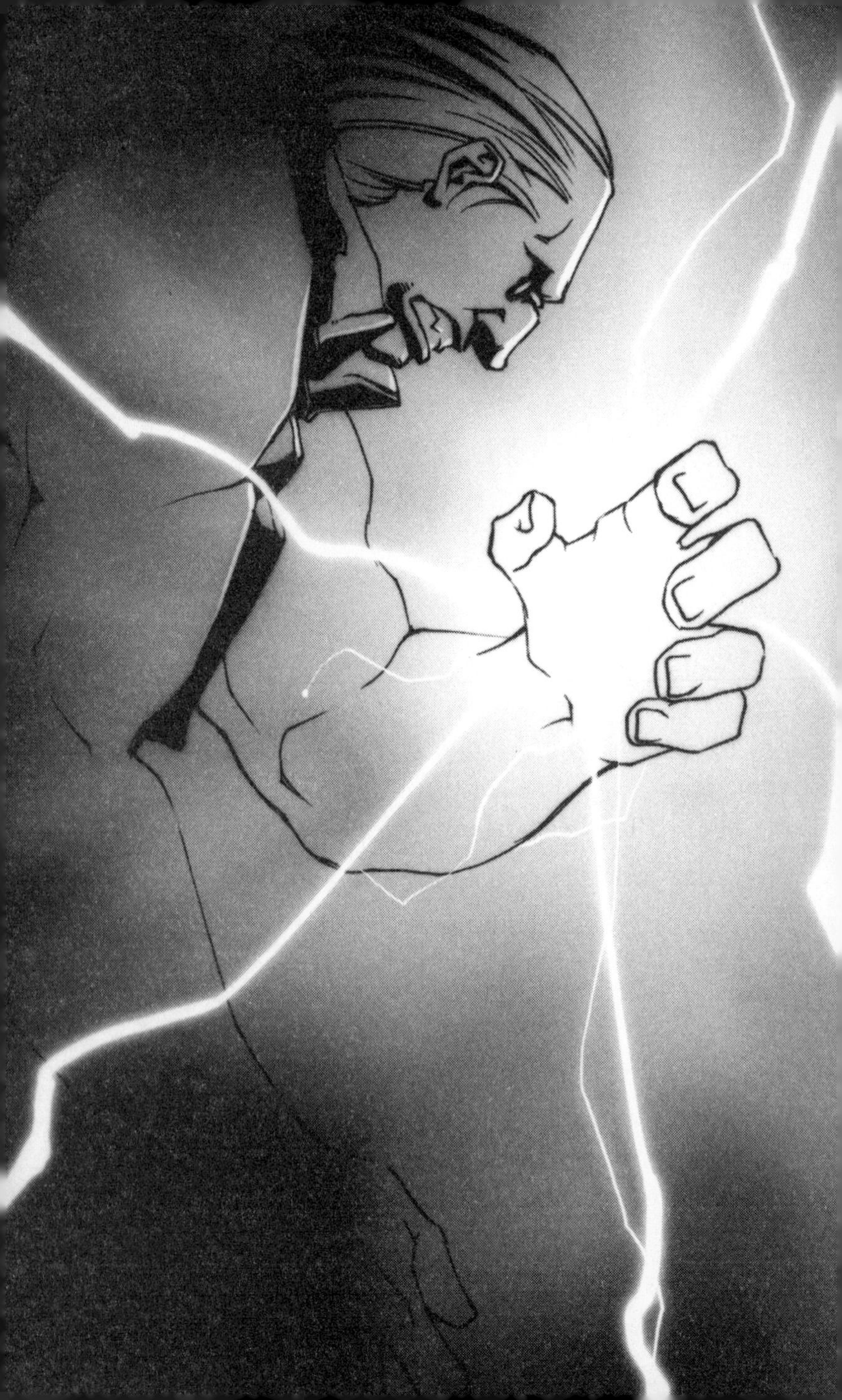

When he first set eyes on the individual who had just transferred into his third year junior high class, Anou Shinjirou felt like someone had grabbed him by the heart. It was love at first sight.

"My name's Taniguchi Masaki. It's nice to meet you all," the new boy said, and gave a gentle smile. Shinjirou thought he was going to fall into those eyes. He could barely breathe; his throat was dry.

But a moment later, all the girls in class shrieked, and he was jolted back to reality.

(What am I *thinking*…?)

Until that moment, Shinjirou had believed himself to be just a normal ordinary boy. No sirree, nothing particularly unusual about him, which is why he didn't understand the feelings being born inside him at that very moment.

"He's not so great…" the guy behind him muttered, watching Taniguchi Masaki grin weakly back at the lovesick, squealing girls.

Shinjirou quickly exclaimed, "Y-yeah, I hate him already." The moment the words left his mouth, he was certain they were true. He hated the guy. That was all.

And yet every time he looked at Masaki, his chest began to pound. What could that mean?

Taniguchi Masaki was still bowing, saying "Hello," and giving everyone a vague, embarrassed smile. Shinjirou didn't think it suited his handsome features at all, but all the girls just kept yelling stuff like "Oh, wow!," and "He's so cute!"

He couldn't stop himself from feeling immensely irritated. The very sight of Masaki giving his feeble little friendly smile was unbearably unpleasant for him.

Shinjirou shouted inside himself, 'Stop doing that! Stop smiling!! It's not right!!!' An incomprehensible urge to strangle Masaki fluttered deep in his heart.

***

Taniguchi Masaki was soon idolized by almost all the girls in the school.

For starters, the boy should have been going to a much better school than this one. On top of that, everyone was right in the middle of exams, so the girls bombarded Masaki all at once with pleas to check their homework. He hardly ever refused, and as a result, he was almost always surrounded by throngs of ladies whenever he was at school.

(Shit…)

Shinjirou spied the action all from the desolate safety of his far corner seat. It was clear that every glare he gave in Masaki's direction was always filled with icy anger and resentment.

If only he could talk to Masaki like that…he found himself thinking.

"Doesn't he just piss you off?" the guy next to him would ask.

"Mm?" he started, turning towards his classmate.

The guy nodded, "I know how you feel, man. Guy pisses me off to no end."

"Y-yeah…" Shinjirou had, somehow, become the boy in school who hated Masaki the most. Despite never having actually fought with him, he'd somehow earned that reputation.

And thus, all the girls hated him.

"What the hell is Anou's problem?"

"Oh, he's just *jealous*."

"Never heard of anything so *pathetic*."

Their whispers were easily overheard, and only served to direct his anger even more.

Even Masaki thought Shinjirou hated him. That blow was the one that hurt Shinjirou the most.

But he still didn't understand his own feelings.

He couldn't work out why Taniguchi Masaki preyed on his mind like this. The conscious knowledge that they were the same gender prevented him from grasping the true nature of his all too obvious emotions. His previous lack of interest in other men besides Masaki was another big reason for his sudden confusion.

His environment didn't give him the latitude to work things

out. Even if he had understood the true nature of his feelings, there was nowhere and no one he could ever go to where those feelings would be accepted.

If his classmates found out, he would be shunned. They didn't even like him much as it was now, but if they knew…he would be considered less than human.

If his parents found out, they'd disown him or worse…haul him off to a psychiatric ward.

Shinjirou's mind was a thunderstorm of confusion and doubt. Fear of the unknown meant he couldn't act on his feelings. And as a result, he made no real attempt to ever sort things out.

But despite his ignorance, the feelings kept surging up inside him, unconsciously causing him pain.

He wanted to talk to Masaki. He wanted to be near him. He didn't know why, but he knew he had no choice.

(Aahhhhhhh…!!!)

Miserable, he began yelling at people for absolutely no reason, he would disobey his teachers at every turn, and he would get into full-blown fist fights over the most trivial things.

Then one day, the pressure got too much for him, and he managed to convince all of his club's *kouhai* into mounting an assault on Masaki. They all had a grudge against "Study Abroad"—Taniguchi Masaki—to begin with, so they didn't need much persuading.

"Heh heh, let's do it."

"That asshole's been on my shit list for a while."

"We'll show him how far his pretty face can take him."

"Good," Shinjirou grinned, but in fact, he was planning to burst onto the scene and rescue Masaki.

He wanted to make friends with him. If this gave him a chance to do that, then he didn't care what crap he had to take from his *kouhai* afterwards—his emotions left him no choice.

This 'strategy' went into motion a few days later after school.

They followed Masaki on his usual trip home, and when Masaki ducked into his usual back alley shortcut to the train station, Shinjirou signaled to his five *kouhai*, "Go for it."

The five boys quickly snuck into the deserted alley. By the time Masaki realized he was being followed, it was too late…he was already surrounded.

"So, Mr. Study Abroad. You've been doing pretty well for yourself, haven't ya?" It was obvious they were trying to sound tough.

But things didn't progress as Shinjirou had originally hoped. He had been so sure that Masaki would be scared out of his wits that he never considered the possibility that maybe, just maybe, Masaki would instead take the scenario in stride and be totally calm and collected. "Right…I'll be more careful," Masaki replied, just standing there and accepting their aggression.

They threatened him, they pushed him, but no matter what they said…his response was completely serene.

(——?)

Watching this from the sidelines, Shinjirou started to fret. Ladies' men weren't supposed to act like this.

Eventually one of his *kouhai* lost his temper and let loose, punching Masaki in the cheek.

(Ah—!)

Shinjirou almost shrieked. He had never planned to let it go that far. He quickly stepped forward, intending to intervene...

But something happened.

A girl appeared, entering the alley from the side opposite to where Shinjirou was hiding.

"Hey," she said, her voice empty, dispassionate. "What is your purpose? What failing of his caused this behavior?" She talked like a windup doll.

(Wh-who the hell is *she*?)

Shinjirou gaped at her, completely blowing the timing of his entrance.

"Hey, this guy thinks he's Don Juan," his *kouhai* snarled, switchblade in hand. "Looking like this, tricking girls into falling for him."

"Huh...so, he stole your girlfriends, then? The cause of your anger is sexual frustration?" What in the world was this girl's problem?!

"Uh...what? What did she say?"

"I'm asking if this attack is a way of forgetting that your sexual partners all hate you."

"You....bitch!"

The situation was rapidly spiraling in a sinister direction. Shinjirou didn't know what to do, and he couldn't force himself out of hiding.

As if things weren't confusing enough already, the girl suddenly tore her own shirt off and stood there bare-chested.

"If you have frustrated desires, I can fulfill them," she said in the most deadpan voice. This girl was out of freaking control.

"Uuuum…"

"H-hey…"

"Whoa! Wait a minute," Masaki yelped, flustered. He had been totally unfazed when he himself was in danger, but once the girl got mixed up in it, his attitude changed.

Watching this, Shinjirou thought, 'Oh, crap!'

He knew he'd made a terrible mistake.

Quickly, he took a step forward, but even as he did, someone even stranger appeared on the scene.

"Well, *this* is easy to figure out!"

A young man in white clothes, positively exuding confidence, strode directly into the alley.

"—! Wh-who are you?!"

"Just to make sure, I'd better ask. You there," he pointed at Masaki. "Do you want to save this girl?"

Masaki nodded, "Y-yes."

"Then take her and run!"

With lightning speed, the man pulled the girl out of the ring of *kouhai* and shoved her towards Masaki.

Taking the man at his word, Masaki took the girl's arm, and fled the scene.

(Wahhh?!)

Shinjirou was horrified. They were running straight towards him.

But they were going too fast, and ran right past him without ever noticing that he was there.

(Wh-what's going on?)

He was a little relieved, but now more confused than ever. Things were playing out in a way that bore no resemblance to his original plans, and he could no longer follow anything.

He looked back at the man in white, and somehow, all his *kouhai* had already been defeated, and were lying in a bloody heap on the ground.

"Eeek!" Shinjirou let out a little shriek, and the man turned towards him.

"Can't say I think much of your methods," the man said, like he had been well aware that Shinjirou had been hiding there all along.

The man smiled. It was a villainous, heartless smile.

"Aaaaugh!" Shinjirou ran for it.

He ran as hard as he could, not stopping until he reached the square by the side of the station.

Feeling safe, he relaxed…and realized that Masaki and the girl were sitting together on a bench on the other side of the square.

"Ah…!" he wailed.

He had been right.

It was obvious that they were drawn to each other. Especially Masaki, whose heart had been stolen by the girl. It was written all over his face. He'd never looked like that at school, all red faced and smiling.

"…………!"

In that very moment, Shinjirou felt all of the energy drain

out of his body.

***

A few days afterwards, Masaki went on a date with the girl. Shinjirou watched from the shadows, having followed Masaki every day since the incident.

(Augh...)

He ground his teeth as he watched the couple head for the movie theater. Masaki appeared to be quite surprised by how crowded the theater was.

They talked for a moment, apparently arguing.

(Oooh...)

Shinjirou waited hopefully. The girl joined the line on her own, leaving Masaki just standing there.

After a moment, Masaki turned and walked towards the main road.

Pleased by this turn of events, Shinjirou quickly followed after him.

Masaki looked all around as he walked, as if searching for some place in particular. With his heart pounding, Shinjirou took this opportunity to walk over to Masaki and speak to him. "Oh, Study Abroad. What are *you* doing here?" His tone was rather aggressive, out of habit.

"Ah, um, you know," Masaki replied, scrunching up his face unhappily.

Shrinking back from this reception, Shinjirou said, "Yeah, I do. You're making some chick wait for you, huh?"

But Masaki just answered, "Sorry, in kind of a hurry," and rushed off.

"Ah…!" Shinjirou wondered where he was going, but Masaki just ducked into a fast food place, and after a few minutes, popped out with a large paper bag and some drinks, and headed back to where the girl was waiting in line.

They began happily munching away on their burgers.

"…………"

As Shinjirou watched vacantly, the girl suddenly kissed Masaki. To be strictly accurate, it wasn't technically a kiss—she had actually licked off a blob of ketchup from Masaki's cheek with her tongue—but to Shinjirou, this sudden display was far more erotic than any old kiss.

"…………"

Shinjirou's face turned white as a sheet. He was trembling.

Unable to take any more, he turned and fled.

***

"Ah, that'd be Orihata. She's in our school, yeah."

Shinjirou had called everyone he knew, trying to find out the girl's name. And now he had it. He had the hateful name of his archenemy's girlfriend—Orihata Aya. The very name only drew more questions. "What's she like?!" he urged.

On the other end of the line, a friend of his from elementary school hesitated, "Um…well…" Then he sniggered, meaningfully.

"You did her, then?"

"Huh? No, nothing like that…"

"Better be careful, man. Everyone knows about Orihata. Hee hee hee."

"What do you mean?"

"She looks all good girl, right? Like some choir chick? Oh, but she's a total slut."

The rude word caught Shinjirou totally off guard. "Wh-what?"

"I know dozens of guys who say they've done her. Hee hee."

"Really?"

"She'll do anyone that asks. Go for it, man. Say her name and she'll follow you anywhere. Course, you gotta watch out that you don't catch somethin' from her…hee hee hee hee."

"_____" Shinjirou couldn't answer.

Did Masaki know about this?

Ever since they'd met, Masaki had appeared more alive, even from a distance, like his life had taken on new meaning. It seemed like he was really in love with her, and that made his every waking moment enjoyable.

Additionally, his previously reluctant reception to the girls who flocked around him shifted, and he spoke to them warmly. Living proof of the old counselor's maxim that the better your life is going, the nicer you are to other people. This made him even more popular than ever, but Shinjirou was way past being jealous of that.

Masaki was in the midst of the kind of love that comes along only once a lifetime…and the girl probably didn't deserve any of it. Surely lurking in his future was a horrendous heartbreak. But what could Shinjirou do?

(—Just leave them be? Yeah, a guy like that deserves to be put through the wringer by some lying, evil bitch!)

Yes, sometimes he thought like that. But at other times, he thought he might be able to take advantage of the situation and somehow get closer to Masaki.

(Auuuugh…)

The test was right on top of them, but Shinjirou never thought of anything but Masaki and Aya, and as a result, his scores plummeted.

He abandoned his studies to do nothing but obsessively follow Masaki—and, of course, Orihata Aya, who was almost always with him. And gradually, he started keeping an even closer eye on Orihata Aya than he did Masaki. He would lie to his parents and tell them he was going to cram school, but in reality, he would venture out and stand outside Orihata's apartment building, beneath the wintry night sky, feeling the north wind slice his body to ribbons.

"Aaugh…"

He had no conscious recognition of how creepy his behavior was. No, he was merely following Orihata Aya because he was desperate to know the truth—why did Masaki like her? But the meaningless irritation pouring out of him prevented him from understanding.

"I'm gonna figure out who she is…" he muttered to himself

in the darkness. The lights in Orihata Aya's room were off.

From Shinjirou's stalker-ish observations, he gathered that Orihata Aya must live alone. He'd never seen any sign of other family members in the apartment, and the lights inside were never left on—whether Orihata Aya was there or not. After a date with Taniguchi Masaki, the lights would go on for about ten minutes, presumably while she was in the shower, but they'd be turned off right afterwards.

Does anyone go to sleep that fast?

At first, his perverted mind thought that she might be doing something naughty, and this fantasy excited him initially—and the knotty mess of that feeling made Shinjirou hate himself even more. But as his observations continued, he realized that this occurrence happened each and every time she came home, like clockwork, and he began to doubt that possibility. No one masturbates like that, not even Shinjirou.

The most troubling thing about these observations was realizing how dull Orihata Aya's life really was. She never watched TV or anything. She just sat there in total darkness. Did this girl even have a private life?

On days when she didn't meet Masaki, she would come directly home from school, go out to buy a *bento* at the convenience store for her dinner, and the lights would go off shortly after she returned home with it. Most of the time, the *bento* was a plain *nori bento*; nothing to spice up her meals at all.

It was like this girl did nothing. She just went through the normal motions of life, but never actually lived it.

(Why would anyone go for an expressionless mannequin of a girl like her...?)

One thing Shinjirou realized quite quickly from his observations was that his friend was a liar. There were no signs of the mythical parade of men his friend had so playfully spoken of. No, there was only Masaki. There were no indications at all of her ever going off with other men, and this left him with absolutely no evidence at all to confront Masaki with.

(Shit...)

Teeth chattering in the cold, Shinjirou carried on stalking her. Had anyone seen him, they would certainly have called the police.

***

Then one night...

Shinjirou was staring up at Orihata Aya's room when the door slid open. The lights inside remained off.

It was really cold, so it couldn't possibly be an attempt to air the place out.

He held his breath, watching, and Orihata Aya came out on the veranda alone...in her underwear.

Her hair was a mess. She looked like she'd just woken up. Didn't she have anything else she could sleep in besides her underwear?

"............"

Silently, the girl put her hands on the railing, and stood there, not moving. She was immobile, stiff, staring down from her veranda.

(.........?)

Shinjirou looked up at her through the binoculars he had with him, and shivered.

Orihata Aya's trademark mask-like face was gone. She was biting her lower lip so hard that it had turned blue, and she was shaking like a leaf. He could tell from the uncanny light shining in her wide-open eyes that it was not because of the cold.

Something was tormenting her...but what?

She looked as though she was about to jump.

(H-hey—)

Shinjirou gulped, but kept watching.

Her lips parted, and she whispered something. The same words, over and over and over.

She kept on whispering and whispering until eventually Shinjirou couldn't stand it any longer. He had to get in closer.

Shinjirou quietly scampered towards the building's outer wall, and it was there, carried on the chilly wind, that her 'spell' reached Shinjirou's ears.

It went as follows:

"I have no right to fall in love. I have no right to fall in love. I have no right to fall in love. I have no right to fall in love. I have no right to fall in love. I have no right to fall in love. I have no right to fall in love. I have no right to fall in love. I have no right to fall in love. I have no right to fall in love. I have no right to fall in love. I have no right to fall in love. I have no right to fall in love. I have no right to fall in love. I have no right to fall in love. I have no right to fall in love. I have no right to fall in love. I have no right to fall in love. I have no right to fall in love…"

On and on and on it went, like she was spitting out blood.

Shinjirou was bewildered.

(Wh-what the hell…is she *saying*?)

He couldn't comprehend it…but deep inside his body something made him shiver, and it wasn't the cold. Something in him had responded to her single-minded intensity. Something perhaps very similar to what Taniguchi Masaki had felt about her.

But it was beyond Shinjirou's capability to understand it.

"So you're the one who's been following Camille around? You got a crush on her…or something?" A voice snarled from behind him.

"——?!" He spun around in shock, but he wasn't quick enough. The hideously fat man behind him—Spooky E—reached out with both his hands and grabbed ahold of the young stalker.

Electricity raced through Shinjirou's body, and he passed out instantly, crumpling to the ground.

"Huh…" Spooky E sneered, picking Shinjirou up in one hand like a shopping bag, and carried him around to the building's garbage dump.

Above them, oblivious to their presence, Orihata Aya struggled desperately to crush her feelings for Taniguchi Masaki, shivering in her underwear, whispering over and over, "…I have no right to fall in love with him…"

***

Spooky E stood in the darkness, hands on the sides of the unconscious Anou Shinjirou's head. His fingers slowly, slowly moved across the boy's scalp.

With each movement, bits of Shinjirou's body would twitch. Once, the ring finger on his left hand curled; another time, his right eyelid opened, then shut.

"O…o…aahhh…" His mouth opened, meaningless sounds spilling out. "O…o…rihata…Orihata…Orihata Aya…"

When the words acquired meaning, Spooky E grinned. He had reached the part of Shinjirou's brain that knew about her.

Spooky E briefly removed his hands, stuck his fingers in his mouth, and licked them all over. Once they were covered in saliva, he placed them back on Shinjirou's head.

Spooky E's hands generated a very low power electromagnetic wave. He could use this to shock the cells in someone's brain, and manipulate their memories and their very psyche. His power was called "Spooky Electric." It was where his code name was derived from. He was a synthetic human. By licking his fingers, he was able to increase the conductivity of the very electromagnetic wave he was generating.

"Okay, Anou Shinjirou. You will no longer pay the slightest attention to that girl or anything to do with her," Spooky E said. He had discovered the boy's name from the student ID card in his pocket.

"I will not."

"From now on, you will have no personal desires," Spooky E whispered, massaging the boy's frontal lobes.

"I will not."

"From now on, you work for the Towa Organization as one of our living terminals."

"I am a terminal."

"The sex drive that troubles you no longer exists," Spooky E's fingers slid between Shinjirou's forehead and his eyes. Hunting for the hypothalamus and the limbic system.

"No sex drive."

"You are no longer lonely."

"Not lonely."

"You don't want a lover…you don't want friends."

"I don't."

These quiet questions and answers continued for another thirty minutes.

Eventually, Spooky E whispered in Shinjirou's ear, "You will enter Shinyo Academy and await instructions."

"I will."

"Programming complete. Reset all systems, reactivate in ten minutes."

"Complete."

And with that, Shinjirou's body toppled over, immobile.

***

"I'm home."

Hearing the voice from the doorway, Anou Kumiko jumped up from the sofa. She had dozed off.

Curiously, that was her son Shinjirou's voice. She hurriedly looked at the clock, but quickly realized that he was home more than an hour earlier than when cram school should have let out. She had not overslept.

"What's wrong, Shin-chan?" she asked. "Did something happen at cram school?"

Her son looked much more relaxed than usual. The closer the test got, the more stressed out he'd become, but that seemed to have vanished.

"No, I quit," he said, calmly.

Kumiko freaked. "EH?! Wh-what's that supposed to mean?"

"My scores have been taking a nose dive. I realized I was going to the wrong school," he answered readily.

"B-but...all on your own? And wasn't it your idea to go in the first place?"

"I switched to a different school. The one by the station." He mentioned the name of a big school that handled college entrance exam students as well.

Kumiko was taken aback, but when she heard that he'd already done all the paperwork and paid for the course fees, she frowned. "With what money?"

"I had some savings."

"How much?"

"Two hundred thousand yen."

She was staggered. She had known he had that kind of money saved up from New Year's presents and the like, but for him to use that money on studying was unthinkable.

"I want to get into a prefectural school, at least," he continued, composedly.

"Sh-Shin-chan..." Kumiko couldn't decide if she should be happy at her son's newfound maturity or to continue freaking out over his rash decisions.

"But first, what's for dinner? I didn't get anything on the way home..."

He ate twice as much as usual.

"Um, Shin-chan?" Kumiko asked, hesitantly.

He looked up from his third bowl of rice. "What?"

"Which school are you thinking about?"

"Shinyo Academy. I should be able to make that level...if I start now."

"You...you really want to?"

"It's worth a shot. I've been dragging my feet way too long, though..." He shook his head.

Kumiko wasn't sure why, but she couldn't stop worrying.

When he finished dinner, he went straight to his room and started studying.

Kumiko snuck a peek, and found him actually at his desk, without the headphones he always had on, plugging away at his study guides and notes.

"............"

She held her breath, unable to tear herself away from the crack in the door. Yet her son never moved, continuing to study away in exactly the same position for hours like he had become some kind of machine.

Eventually her husband came home, and Kumiko hurriedly told him what was happening.

"Mm? Sounds great. Finally found some motivation."

"But there's something strange about him. Like…oh, I can't put it into words…" She must have looked very high strung at that moment.

Her husband frowned in irritation. "Come off it. You're his mother. He's the one taking the test. You put too much pressure on him and he won't be able to concentrate," he snapped.

"Yes, I know, but…"

"Sounds like you've got a case of exam nerves. Just take a deep breath and relax, dear."

"Okay…" Kumiko nodded in agreement. It *was* true that she wanted him to study more, and she couldn't deny that the current developments were a bit of a relief. And really, it wasn't *that* strange…

And with that, the intuitive doubt that had arisen inside her was washed away in a flood of sensible analysis.

***

General opinion of Anou Shinjirou abruptly improved. Everyone noticed that he had become more serious. This more motivated turn not only impressed the teachers, but also softened the views of his classmates. Most of all, everyone kept expressing surprise at his sudden lack of interest in Taniguchi Masaki.

"Well, I thought about it, and realized I was just jealous. And you know, that's really not cool…" Shinjirou said, and since Masaki's number one enemy had changed his mind, the other guys began to think differently as well, and soon none of them were openly bad mouthing Taniguchi Masaki.

The first group to come around was the very girls that had treated him like an insect before. "Huh…Anou-kun's not a bad guy after all…"

"All that conflict between him and Masaki-kun was just some stupid rivalry…" they said, spinning things positively all on their own.

Taniguchi Masaki himself was probably the only person who didn't pick up on the sea of change. His head was full of Orihata Aya, and he had no time for anything else.

Anou Shinjirou himself cared little for the reaction it provoked. He was simply plugging away at his studies, gradually getting closer to the benchmark for the high school he was aiming for.

"Well, Anou, you're doing very well. You should have no problem at all getting into Shinyo Academy," his teacher said, during one of their counseling sessions.

"But I can't slack off now," Shinjirou replied calmly.

"Hey, that's my line! Ha ha ha! But true, very true. Keep up the good work."

"Yes."

"You're living proof that all you have to do is put your mind to it. Don't think about anything else; just concentrate and you'll get there."

"I think so too," Shinjirou nodded quietly.

But his teacher frowned at him. "Hey…is something wrong?"

"What?"

"You're crying."

"Huh?" Shinjirou put his hand to his eyes. His cheeks were wet. "I am? But why?" he murmured.

"You getting enough sleep? I mean, I'm glad you're working so hard, but maybe you ought to try and take things a little easier now."

"…………"

But Shinjirou had no answer. He just sat there, tears rolling down his cheeks, staring into space, unable to understand why he was crying.

***

"Dear Anou Shinjirou-kun,

I'm sorry to send you a letter like this so suddenly. I know this is a busy time for everyone, and no one has time to spare, but I have something I need to say to you.

I think I'm in love with you.

Is that strange? I don't even know my own feelings. I know I softened the sentiment with a dumb phrase like, "I think," but that's the truth of it.

Until just a while ago, I was like everyone else, and totally misunderstood you. You just seemed to always be angry about something, so it was hard to ever get near you. But..."

"........."

This letter was resting in his shoe locker when he left school. When he opened the letter, a whiff of perfume emerged. The paper was soaked in it. He started reading the letter with no reaction at all, and soon he realized it was a love letter.

"But recently, I started watching you, and I realized that you were only angry because the true nature of your feelings was not being understood.

Am I right? I'm sure I am. I understand...because I feel the same way.

I know I might be making this all up, but I feel like you're the only one who can understand my feelings. I hate to trouble you, but will you meet me? Just this once?

Please give me a chance..."

The letter continued, giving a date, time and place to meet... but no name.

"........." Shinjirou remained expressionless, just standing there holding the letter. He didn't know what to do, so he remained motionless.

Eventually, he moved stiffly over to a nearby phone booth.

Automatically, he dialed the number implanted in his brain.

The call was answered the moment it connected.

"State your name," the high-pitched voice on the other end

of the line said.

"D1229085. Urgent communication for Spooky E," Shinjirou said, in a flat, mechanical tone.

"What, something happened?"

"Emergence of Emotional Circuit Response Case F. Disturbance level A."

The man on the other end of the line clicked his tongue in irritation. "Report details."

Shinjirou did so mechanically.

When he finished, the voice said, "Hmm. So this girl was drawn to a loner like you? Go for it, take her invitation. I'll permit it."

"Understood. Permission received."

"Where did she want to meet?"

Shinjirou told him, and Spooky E made a pleased chuckle. "Rather a lonely place for a romantic tryst, mm? Bet you anything that girl wants you to do her. Hee hee hee hee."

"............."

"Okay, that place might do just fine, but if it looks like there are other people around, try and lure her out to some place deserted. I'll 'condition' her."

".........."

"Do you understand?"

"I understand."

"Okay, when you hang up the phone you will return to normal mode in twelve seconds. You will forget about the letter until it is time for the meeting."

"I understand. I will hang up."

He hung up, put the letter in his bag, stood for a few seconds absently, and when he hit the twelve second mark, snapped out of it, and left the school, heading for his cram school, same as he always did.

He sat through classes like always, and during the short lull between classes, he found a spot on a bench in the rest area and ate a hamburger.

Around him were several children his age, and a group of high school kids studying for college.

Right next to Shinjirou, one such girl said, "Oh god, what *is* this? Help me, Suemaaa!"

"Touka! At this stage of the game, you *have* to know *this*!"

"I know, but…"

The two girls were studying together. Their uniforms were obviously from Shinyo Academy, which is where he was planning to go to high school, but he paid them no attention.

"………" While he ate, he flipped through his vocabulary book.

But his hand stopped for a moment.

His gaze was drawn to a painting hung on the wall opposite him.

It was a painting of a great crowd of people sitting in a waste-land, holding hands. There were several black goats around them, eating the rose bushes that grew in the wilderness.

"…………" He couldn't take his eyes off it.

Eventually the bell rang, and everyone got up and went back to their classrooms, but Shinjirou just sat there, motionless.

Left alone, as if frozen to his seat.

"............."

Ever since Spooky E had "conditioned" him, Shinjirou had stopped thinking on his own. He simply followed the implanted instructions and the expectations of those around him, dutifully.

So why was he unable to respond to this painting, like he had been nailed to the floor?

"............" He stared up at the painting.

From behind him, a voice said, "What you are experiencing is what we call 'emotion.'"

Shinjirou turned around. Behind him stood a young man in white clothes.

"Uh…" He could swear he'd seen the guy somewhere before, but he couldn't remember where. Yet he *had* seen him. Where was it…?

The man seemed to think they hadn't spoken before. At the previous meeting, the man had been unable to see Shinjirou, so he didn't recognize him. Neither one of them knew that they were meeting for the second time.

"Your heart was moved by something in that painting. But you've had no such experience in your life before, so you had no sample data inside to tell you how to react," the man in white said quietly, walking towards Shinjirou.

"............" Shinjirou said nothing. He was unable to react to this man as well.

"You're Anou Shinjirou, right? From the public school last minute preparation course?" The man in white sat down next to

Shinjirou.

"Yes, I am."

"My name is Asukai Jin. I'm in charge of the national art school preparation course here. I've had my eye on you, Anou-kun." He smiled gently.

"Why?" Shinjirou asked.

The man raised one eyebrow, as if joking. "You probably don't know."

"Know what?"

"That you have absolutely no hope," he said, calmly, but with a trace of sadness.

"What does that mean...?" Shinjirou asked.

But the man didn't answer. He stood up, slowly turned his back, and whispered, "The man who played with your heart worked for the Towa Organization, correct?"

This word was implanted deep inside Shinjirou. The moment he heard it, his body moved automatically.

His lungs screamed at the sudden motion, but he ignored them, flinging his body towards the man.

Even though his back was turned, the man stepped lightly to one side, easily dodging Shinjirou's lunge.

Shinjirou's body was carried onwards, flying into the tables and chairs opposite.

There was a huge crashing sound.

Bleeding from several places, Shinjirou sprang to his feet again. There was no trace of emotion on his face.

His head turned, looking for the man.

The man did not run, but instead, he stood his ground.

"Hmph…" A cruel smile appeared on his lips.

Shinjirou—or rather the body being controlled by implanted instructions— launched himself towards the man again.

This time, he grabbed the man. He pushed him over, and tried to put one arm around his neck to strangle him.

But before he could, the man's hand reached out to Shinjirou's chest.

"_____!"

A moment later, Shinjirou's body suddenly bent over of its own accord, and flung itself backwards.

There was another tremendous crash.

"Pathetic…" the man said, unmoved. He stood up, and brushed the dust off his clothes.

He came over to where Shinjirou lay unable to move, and got down on his knees. He peered into the boy's face.

"What was that sound?"

"Asukai-san, what happened?"

Several other faculty members had come running.

"He fell over. Looks like anemia of the brain…" Asukai replied, helping Anou Shinjirou up, and over to a comfortable sofa, where he laid him down flat.

"Is he okay? Should I call an ambulance?"

"Better ask the manager. If he lies down for a minute…he should be okay, I think…" Asukai answered, well aware that an ambulance pulling up to the cram school was hardly a desirable event.

"W-wait right there, I'll go ask," and the other teachers ran off.

Once again the lobby fell silent, if only for a short while.

"………" Asukai Jin slowly rubbed Anou Shinjirou's chest. "I've no idea of the true nature of your suffering, Anou-kun. But I promise you, your wordless pain will be buried when the snow falls in April…when the whiteness falls on all mankind," he whispered kindly, yet firmly.

Behind him, floating in the air, a vision of a girl wavered.

***

When Shinjirou awoke, he was lying on a sofa at his cram school. His mother was sitting next to him, peering at his face with a worried expression. Apparently, someone had called her.

"Shin-chan, how do you feel?"

"…Umm…wh-where…?"

"Cram school. You…you passed out," his mother said.

He looked around him. Everything felt strange, like his eyes wouldn't quite focus.

"Cram school…" he got to his feet unsteadily. He stood there, looking puzzled.

"Should we go see a doctor?" his mother asked.

But he didn't appear to be seriously injured, so they simply headed straight home. They went for a check up the next day, but the doctors found nothing amiss. For safe measure, they gave him a mild tranquilizer, and then just sent him home. The diagnosis was simply stress. He had been studying far too much.

"Thank goodness."

"Yeah…"

"The test is pretty close, but you don't need to work too hard. The teachers all agree…you'll do fine."

"Yeah…"

***

When they got home, Shinjirou did as the doctors had suggested and went to bed.

He awoke soon after, and stood up. He reached for his bag, untouched since he'd come home the day before, and emptied it out onto his bed. He planned to reorganize the contents by priority.

Text books, study guides, notes…and a letter he didn't remember getting.

"…………"

As tempting as the letter was, he did not open it. He simply stood there, holding it in his fingers, looking off into nothing.

***

Two tall office buildings and a department store that housed a number of specialty shops had been piled on top of each other into one giant complex known as the Twin City. It was one of the many areas planned for during the redevelopment of the station area, and the only one completed yet.

On a daily basis, tens of thousands of people came here.

Customers for the department store, businessmen with deals to be done—they all flooded in and out of the building in a constant stream.

But once a month, on the third Wednesday, the department store would close for the day, and the place would be completely and utterly deserted...just a vast, empty space. The business hotel's rent was far too expensive, and it had hardly any tenants.

The roof of the department store was open to the eighth and ninth floors of the tenant buildings. This 'connection space' was also deserted that day. The department store was closed, but the elevators in the office buildings were operating, so the roof was still accessible. The game centers and *yakisoba* shops that catered to the passing businessmen were all closed, and nothing visited but the wind.

And still, this monthly void in the middle of the city was where the girl in the letter promised to meet Anou Shinjirou.

At four in the afternoon, the sun was already setting, painting the world red.

The elevator that on any other day stopped at nearly every floor took him directly to his destination.

"............"

There was a gust of wind as Shinjirou came onto the roof. It was always windy this high up, but today exceptionally so. One of the screens used to break the wind had come loose, and was flapping noisily, but there was nobody here to fix it.

"Um...hello?" Shinjirou looked around him, searching for signs of life. There was nobody there, no signs of anybody having been there.

The meeting spot was in the center of the rooftop, near some round, squarish, enigmatic sort of abstract sculptures. Shinjirou headed towards them.

Long shadows spread out like stripes across the floor. A girl was seated alone on one of the sculptures.

"You…you wrote the letter…?"

"………" The girl nodded, silently. She wore a thick navy blue coat, and a thick wool hat. Her hair was bound in two braids, and she wore glasses.

He'd never seen her before.

"Um…so, what did that letter mean?" Shinjirou asked.

"…………" She didn't answer. She just stared at the ground.

Shinjirou made no attempt to approach, stopping a good distance from her.

"I thought someone was making fun of me at first, but you're actually here…"

"……………"

"But when did you put the letter in my bag? I don't remember leaving it lying around…"

"—What?" The girl's face snapped up. For a moment, the setting sun glinted off her glasses. "What did you just say?" Her voice sounded more like a boy's.

"Huh?"

"*You found the letter in your bag? That's why you came here?*"

"What about it?" Shinjirou stared at her blankly.

She suddenly yelled, "*Look out!*" and dove towards Shinjirou, knocking him aside.

"Waah—?!"

A moment later, something black and round cut through the air where Shinjirou had been standing.

The impact of its landing shook the roof, and then it stood up—Spooky E.

The monstrous man had planned to crush Shinjirou on his dive. But he had failed.

"——?!"

Spooky E swung his fist towards the girl who had spotted his attack.

But his punch met only fabric—the girl had tossed her coat, and was no longer there.

Instead, her hat and glasses spun in the air, falling to the floor of the roof.

Something like a thick black rope landed on top of them—the braids that had emerged from under her hat. They were fake.

"What—?!" Spooky E yelled, stomping on the glasses and fake braids, glaring around him.

There was no sign of the girl—it was questionable if she even was a girl.

"…………" Shinjirou stayed on the ground, making no sound.

Spooky E turned towards him. "How the hell did you escape from my control?"

"Er…"

"You said you found the letter in your bag…but I made you

forget that letter. So how did you find it again?! You should've only come here because I ordered you to!"

"W-what?" Shinjirou had no idea what the man was shouting about. He'd never seen him before in his life.

Spooky E reached his hand towards Shinjirou. Something flashed in the air between them.

"_____!"

Spooky E yanked his hand back quickly. But it was too late; there was already a long, thin cut on his arm, deep enough to draw blood.

A microfilament wire.

It had moved at a frightening speed, and sliced open Spooky E's arm the same way a copy paper can sometimes slice your fingers. Worst of all, it had prevented him from getting close to Anou Shinjirou.

From somewhere around them came a whistle. Shinjirou had no taste for classical music, so he didn't know the tune, but it was "Die Meistersinger von Nurnberg."

"You're not nearly as tough as the Manticore," a voice said. Just like the girl, it was an androgynous voice, impossible to tell if it was male or female.

"Wh-what are you?" Spooky E spun around, and found a black shadow standing on one of the sculptures, cloak flapping in the wind.

Its left hand was on its head, holding its pipe-shaped hat as if it had just put it on.

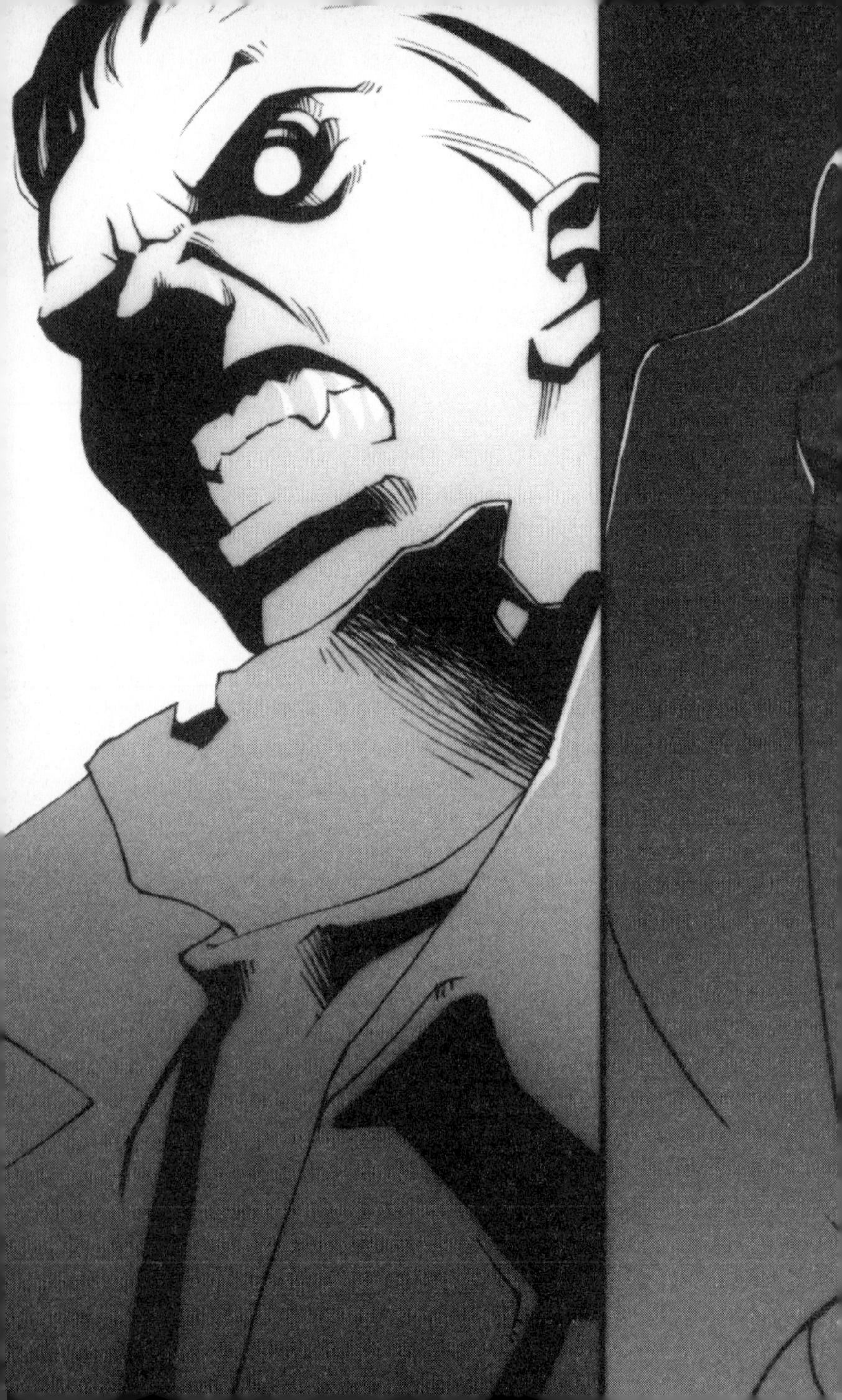

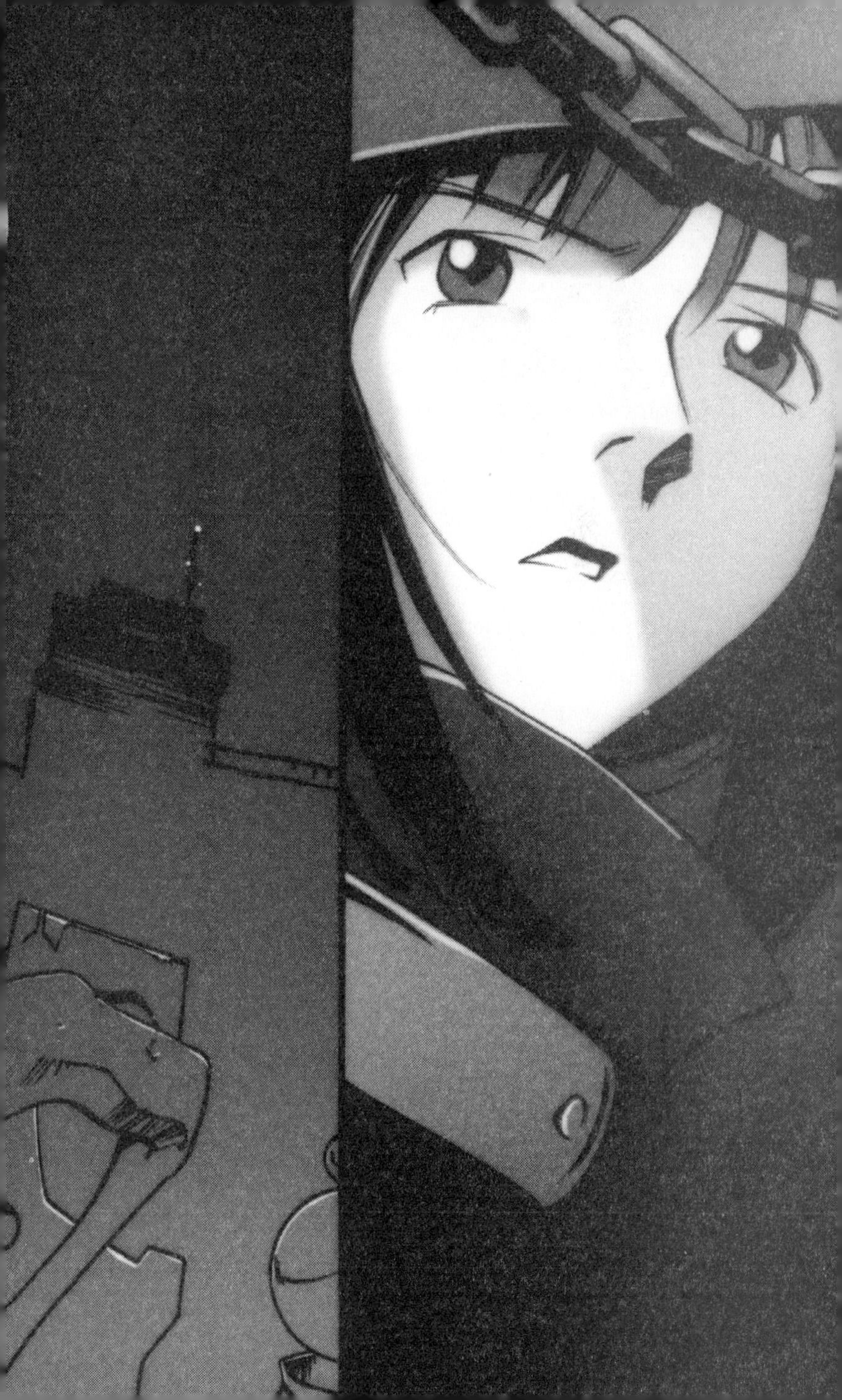

"You should know who I am by now. After all, you are one of the Towa Organization's synthetic humans." The cloaked figure brushed its fingers across its lips, leaving them covered in black lipstick. It was as if this figure was performing some sort of magic trick.

The figure let out a strange, asymmetrical expression.

"Y-you're Boogie…!" Spooky E started to scream, then suddenly flinched, leaping backwards. "Unnh!"

Something glinted in the air, following him.

A piece of paper blowing in the wind was neatly sliced in two.

Frantically, Spooky E rolled away, then forced himself upright, pulling a small gun from his pocket and firing at the cloaked figure.

The figure leapt away a moment before the gun was aimed. There was a crunch, and bits of the statue shattered as the bullet ricocheted off of it.

The cloaked figure slid nimbly from shadow to shadow, between the statues.

"Shit shit shit!" Spooky E yelled, firing into the darkness. There was a silencer on the end of the gun, and it made only a vacant, hollow whistle as it fired.

"My primary objective is the Imaginator's reemergence. I should not be bothering with the likes of you," that creepy voice echoed from somewhere.

"But with one of your victims right in front of me, I can hardly ignore matters. I do apologize for the second class treatment, but I'm going to have to destroy you."

"Grrrrrr!" Spooky E ground his teeth.

There was a click as the hammer struck an empty chamber. He tried to reload, but a wire came undulating through the air, wound around the gun, and pulled it from his hand.

"_____!"

"Are you ready?" the voice whispered, seemingly right in his ear.

"S-screw this!" Spooky E turned his back and ran headlong in the opposite direction from where the cloaked figure had last been, in a mad attempt to flee the roof.

In front of him, Anou Shinjirou was still sprawled out on the ground.

Shinjirou lifted his head and yelped, "Uh oh…!" Just the sight of Spooky E running back towards him was enough for him to pull himself together. He scrambled to his feet, and tried to run…

But something grabbed his ankle from behind.

"Augghh!"

"You can't get away from me, boy!" Spooky E yanked Shinjirou towards him, but there was the shrill sound of something slicing through the air…

Spooky E ducked his head, a moment too late.

There was an unpleasant squishing sound.

Spooky E's right ear was torn clean off his head, spinning through the air.

"Naaaaaarrgghhh——!!!"

But Spooky E did not waver. He spun Shinjirou's body, and flung him right towards the flapping windbreaker, where a gaping hole opened onto the fifty meter drop.

"Waaaugggh?!" Shinjirou screamed.

As he flew, he thought over and over, 'This is a dream! This is a dream!'

He refused to believe his life would end like this.

A newspaper headline fluttered across his mind's eye.

'Junior High Student Buckles Under Exam Pressure, Commits Suicide.'

Everyone would be talking about him, saying stuff like, "He was always worried," and, "He couldn't handle the stress."

And they'd all be wrong.

The idea that he died from getting mixed up in a fight between two mysterious inhuman creatures was just beyond imagining. None of them would ever guess.

He would die alone…misunderstood.

(N-no! I don't want *that*!)

From the bottom of his heart, he knew.

He had still not done anything of any real worth.

He screamed something, but he couldn't catch the meaning of his own words. He might have begged for help, but what did he think would help him? His scream did not even reach his own ears—

***

Suddenly, he felt his arm twist violently backwards, his body forcefully thrust in a very different direction. Like a bungee cord reaching its length, he was shot back up into the air, and yank onto the roof.

He landed awkwardly on his back, and let out a howl of pain.

Still beside himself with panic, he stared up at the black figure perched on the edge of the roof. Had it saved him? Or just deflected the enemy's attack?

"…………"

The setting sun behind it kept him from seeing its expression. A strong gust of wind blew its cloak around, but failed to move the figure itself.

Glumly, it whispered, "He got away…"

Shinjirou looked around, but the hideously fat man who had raved incomprehensible things at him was nowhere to be seen.

"Oh well…at least he won't go near you again. He knows if he does, there's surely a risk of crossing paths with me again."

The cloaked figure came towards him. It was shorter than he'd thought at first.

But now that he thought about it, the girl who had been waiting for him was actually this guy in disguise, so of course he was tiny.

Then the letter had all just been a ruse to draw out the mysterious blubberball?

"………" He stared vacantly up at the cloaked figure.

Halfway to him, the cloaked figure bent over and picked something up off of the ground. It was the blubberball's ear, freshly severed. The cloaked figure tossed it lightly into the air, like he'd picked up a ten-yen coin.

"How did you get out from under his control? That's what interests me the most. Although, if I ask, I doubt you'll know. They'd hardly leave such an obvious clue."

Shinjirou was unable to grasp any meaning from those words.

The cloaked figure stopped just in front of him, reached into its cloak, and pulled out not an ear, but a letter.

"This is the real letter. You should have it. The meeting is not for today, but for the day after tomorrow. Make sure to be there," the figure instructed as it handed over the letter to Shinjirou. "I apologize for infringing on your privacy, but will you forgive me? I had no choice."

He took the letter absently, and opened it. It was in the same handwriting, and had the same words. Only the date was different.

"What does this mean?" he asked, looking up.

But the cloaked figure was gone.

There was nothing left but the wind.

***

Two weeks later, Anou Shinjirou passed the entrance exam for Shinyo Academy.

VI

Not all confusion will ever be cleared up.
Sometimes it will solidify, still confused,
and attempt to judge the world.
Like a curse, affecting the world with no
rhyme or reason...

—**Kirima Seiichi** (*VS Imaginator*)

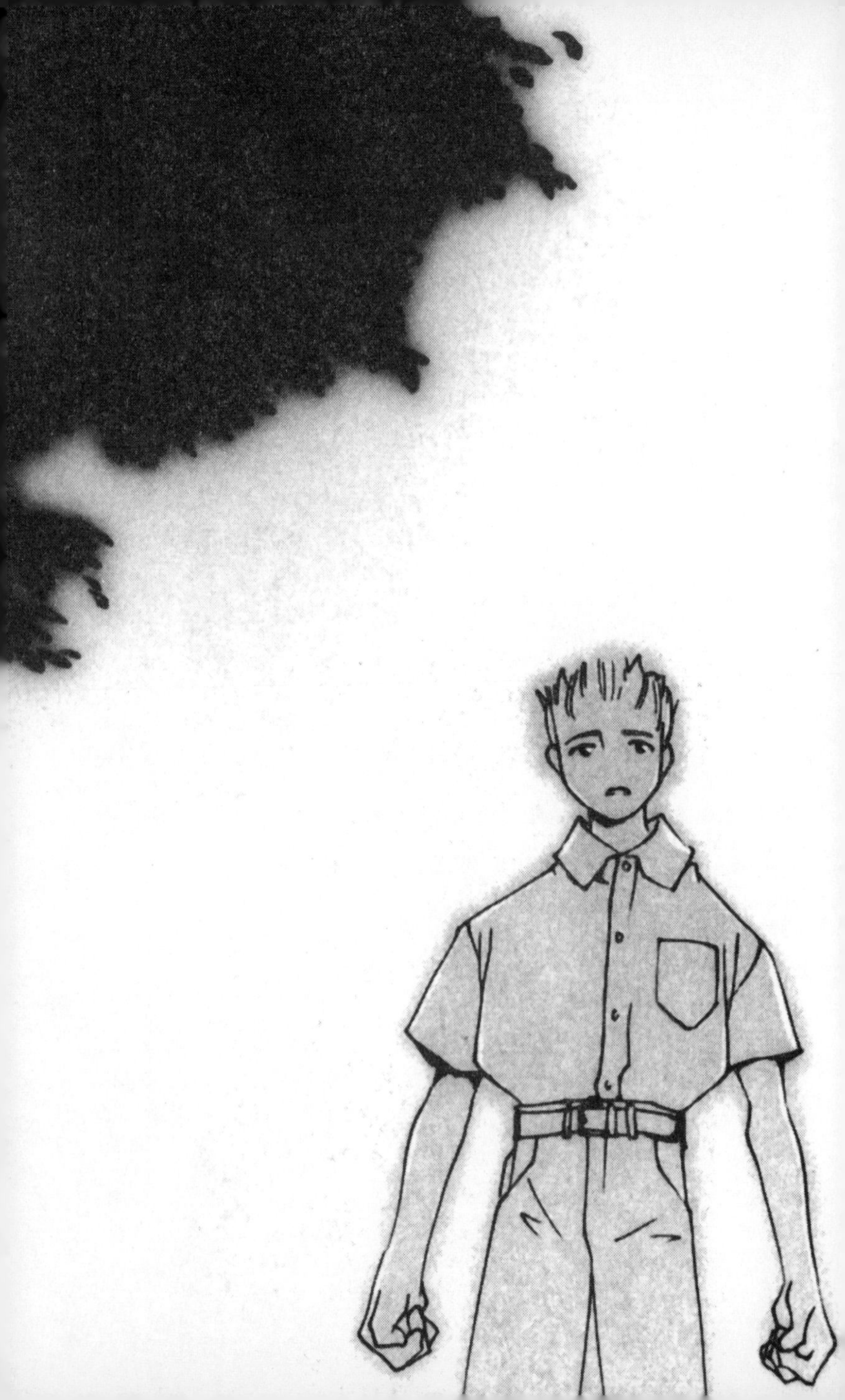

"Please, Suema-san. Save Jin-niisan…"

I couldn't get Kinukawa Kotoe's earnest appeal out of my head. And Asukai Jin's strange behavior at the cram school…that drawing of the girl who killed herself.

I couldn't forget. Even if it wasn't someone like me, a recovering abnormal psychological behavior addict, I don't think anyone else would be able to distance themselves from the matter that easily.

Early in the morning the day after Kinukawa Kotoe had made her request, I went to the place where Minahoshi Suiko had killed herself. It was spring vacation, so I thought the place would be empty, but there was quite a crowd around the gates.

"What's going on?" I wondered.

My friend Miyashita Touka had come with me. "You know, new students getting fitted for uniforms, and handing out the ID cards. You know, orientation crap," she said.

"Oh, yeah." Come to think of it, two years before, we had done the exact same thing. I had completely forgotten.

They all looked like they were having fun. That wouldn't last long. Soon they would be back to the stress of exams, or job hunting, like we were.

"Not the mood for checking out a suicide, is it?" Touka said. "What do you think, Suema? You can go home if you like. I gotta swing by the library."

The reason she'd come with me was something about a book she'd forgotten to return. Wanted to get it back early before we had to head to cram school.

"Nah, I'll come with you."

"Okay then. Ah…" Touka made a face as we reached the gates. "That girl's here. Dang it!"

"Mm? Who?" This was unusual. Touka was not the kind of girl who disliked people easily or avoided them.

"Discipline committee president," she muttered, glumly.

I was even more surprised. "Really? Niitoki-san? But she's so nice!"

"Nah, it's all me. This and that." She put her palms together. "Sorry, gotta go!" she yelled, turning her back and darting off.

"B-but…?!" I stammered, abandoned.

'Oh well,' I thought, as I turned back towards the school.

The new first year students were all happily gathered around the gates, which as anyone who's ever visited our school would know, are set up with gate checks like those found at a train station. You have to actually run your ID card through it just to get in. It's completely useless! And here all the new kids were just "oohing" and "aahing" over it! If you looked really closely though, you could see only about half of them were actually excited about it, while the rest seemed pretty darn alarmed by it.

"Excuse me, coming through," I said, pushing my way towards the gates.

"Morning, Suema-san," said the apparently problematic discipline committee president, Niitoki Kei. We've known each other since we were first year students.

"Morning. You get roped into this just because you're president?" I asked.

She laughed. "I'm not president anymore. But even so…"

"Ah, right, your term's over. It just seemed like something you'd do…"

"What's that supposed to mean?"

"I mean, you know, the big sister thing."

"Pot calling the kettle, Doctor."

We looked at each other and laughed.

"So what brings you here, Suema-san?"

I couldn't answer. It wasn't something to tell just anyone about. "Um…just, you know, *stuff*."

"That Miyashita-san with you?" she said, suddenly.

I was taken aback. "Uh…um, well…"

"She doesn't want to talk to me, huh?"

"Yeah…what's going on there? You two don't seem like you'd rub each other the wrong way…"

"Nah, that's not it. Just, uh…this and that," Kei said, meaningfully and a little forlornly.

"Is this about a boy?" I asked, on a hunch.

Kei's eyes nearly popped out of her head. She gave a nervous giggle. "…You're scary sometimes, you know that? Like you can read my mind."

"Oh…I didn't mean to…" I scrambled.

But it seemed like she didn't take it that badly, and she said pretty lightly, "Bingo. Her boyfriend turned me down. No room for doubt…just clear and direct."

"Oh, the designer guy?"

I'd met him. He was…well, not a bad guy…but that was about the extent of my impression. I think there's something about your friends' boyfriends that makes them hard to get to know.

"Right, that one," Kei said, somehow refreshed.

She was free now, I realized. She'd let him go. I was impressed. I doubt I would manage my heartbreak so neatly. I bet I'd be dragged around by it for ages, but here Kei had already put it behind her.

"If only Touka could be so relaxed about it," I muttered.

Kei laughed. "If only that were all of it. If only that were all."

"Eh? There's more?"

"I know who that girl really is," she said, naughtily.

"Uh…wha?" I asked, but the buzzer on the gate went off.

"Sorry," Kei said, and turned towards the noise.

There was a boy standing in front of the gate, looking blank. He had forgotten to run his card through.

"What's wrong?" Kei asked him.

"Ah…nothing," he said, like his eyes weren't focusing.

The other kids were starting to cluster around.

"You all go on ahead, find your classrooms," Kei said, loudly. Her manner brooked no questions, and everyone did exactly as they were told. She had more authority than most of the teachers.

Kei pulled the boy over to the side. One girl followed him. "What's wrong, Anou-kun?" she asked, worriedly, putting her hand on his shoulder. They wore the same uniform. Looked like they were a couple moving up from the same junior high.

I don't know why, but I thought to myself how nice it must be to be a carefree youth. I was a little jealous.

"N-no…just, um…" Anou-kun stuttered, apparently shaking his head.

"_____"

I knew it was nosy, but I couldn't stop watching them.

"…I just thought, why am I *here*?" Anou-kun said, like nothing made sense to him.

"What do you mean?" Kei asked, puzzled.

"I just…I feel like I lost something really, really important to come here. I don't know what…" Anou-kun muttered.

"Are you okay?"

"Anou-kun had a rough time last year," his girlfriend said.

But he just carried on, like he hadn't even heard her. "I can't figure out what it is. I haven't lost anything. I know that. I know that, but…I don't know what it was, but it was really important. The first time I'd found it…" It was like he was delirious.

Then tears started pouring down his cheeks.

I was surprised, and so were Kei and Anou-kun's girlfriend.

"W-what? What's wrong?"

"Anou-kun?"

"Huh?" He looked up, apparently surprised by his own tears.

He rubbed his cheeks, amazed. "Why am I crying?" he asked, bemused.

I moved away. I just couldn't watch anymore without feeling guilty.

***

I went around the back of the school. It was quiet. There was no one else around.

Just to be on the safe side, I looked around, making sure that I couldn't be seen.

"Okay…"

I clambered up and over the railings of the locked fire escape behind the school. This was the only route left to the roof these days. The door to the roof from the inside set of stairs was locked, and you couldn't get outside. It was locked because Minahoshi Suiko had jumped off the roof, killing herself.

The fire escape made a racket as I climbed, surprising me, so I put my feet down as softly as possible.

It was windy on the roof. Keeping my hair out of my eyes, I headed towards the spot where Minahoshi Suiko had jumped.

I knew I would gain nothing by coming up here. I'm not Sherlock Holmes. I can't claim that a simple visit to the scene will tell me everything, my dear Watson.

But I hoped I would at least catch a feeling.

To be honest, despite all the books I'd read on abnormal psychology, I didn't know squat about suicides.

Of course, I had read interviews with the survivors of botched suicide attempts, but that was ultimately just the words of people who *didn't* die. More than half of those people made no further attempt at suicide, and just went on with their lives.

But those who actually succeeded must be dramatically different. For example, I had read an essay by a writer who had been involved in a number of attempted suicides before finally managing to die. He wrote, "I myself do not particularly want to die, but I am pulled along by my obsession with the woman." Then when he did manage to die, it was in a botched display of attempted suicide which apparently succeeded.

But the real deal, the ones that intentionally die…even if they leave a note, it feels to me like they die without ever really communicating the true reason.

But what about Minahoshi Suiko?

Was she for real? Or was it a failure? Or had everyone misunderstood her, and it was only an accident? Or even worse, was it actually…

I shivered as I walked slowly forward. Then…as I reached the spot, I nearly shrieked. "————?!"

There was a girl standing there, hands on the railings, with a face so desperate she looked like she was about to jump right then and there.

***

Orihata Aya never asked Spooky E why she suddenly had to go to Shinyo Academy.

Even if she had, she could hardly have disobeyed, and as far as tests went, she had enough academic ability implanted in her to pass any test put in front of her, so that was no problem.

"............"

She had come for the new students' orientation, but there was still some time left before it started, so she had gone up to the roof. She wanted to see the sky. Why the gate was barred, she didn't know, but she simply climbed right on over it.

Since she met Taniguchi Masaki, she had begun to like looking up at the sky. When they were walking together, he would often say, "Gosh, the sky sure is beautiful." And sure enough, she had begun to think it was.

"..............."

When she looked at the sky, she felt like her body was melting, like things would be easier.

She sometimes almost believed Masaki might forgive her...

"............"

But that was impossible.

It was unforgivable.

When she thought of all the danger she had put him in, how she had deceived him, how she had kept him from the truth…she could hardly complain, even if he killed her.

Somewhere deep inside, Aya wanted Masaki to kill her.

She thought, 'If that happened, what a weight off my shoulders that would be.'

Before she knew it, she was gripping the railing around the roof tightly, shaking like a leaf.

"Uh…um," a voice stuttered from behind her.

She turned around, and a girl from this high school, her *sempai*, was coming hesitantly towards her.

Aya remembered her face. She had seen her before. Not directly, but in a file. Her name was Suema Kazuko.

"Yes?" Aya asked.

"No, um…I know I might have read things wrong and this may just sound stupid, but…" Suema Kazuko ventured. "But, um, if you're thinking about jumping, then, uh, please don't. Someone already jumped from there. And…and that's not good…"

"………" Aya's eyes widened.

"I…I know there's no guarantee that things will get better if you live, so it's too simple to say so. But, I mean, if you die, then the things you hate, and all those things you can't tolerate…they won't go away. So, uh, my point is…"

While Suema was rambling, she closed the gap between them, and suddenly grabbed ahold of Aya's arm.

Aya looked at that powerful grip, and then at the other girl's face.

"Dying is useless. That's all I can say," Suema said forcefully, staring directly into Aya's eyes. She showed no signs of letting go.

"…………." Aya had no idea of how to clear up the misunderstanding.

Was it really a misunderstanding?

Had she, deep down, really wanted to jump?

She wasn't sure.

But either way, Suema Kazuko probably wouldn't let go. She was sure of that.

"Useless…?" Aya said, quietly.

"Yep. Perhaps you think your life doesn't have any meaning, but dying has even less."

"…………"

Was that true? If she died here, then at least Masaki would be protected, indirectly.

Aya hung her head.

"I want to die," she said, letting herself say it.

Suema frowned. "Really?"

Aya nodded weakly.

"I see. But you can't now…because I found you."

Suema pulled on her arm, dragging Aya to the center of the roof. She forced her to sit down.

"I'm sorry, Suema-san," Aya whispered.

Mm? Suema looked at her, startled. "You know me?"

'Oops,' Aya thought, but her conditioned reflexes took over, and she said smoothly, "Yes, I know someone who goes here. They told me about you. You are Suema Kazuko-sempai, right?"

"Who…? What did you hear? Oh, nah, never mind. I can guess," Kazuko said ruefully, a little exasperated.

"I'm sorry."

In fact, her photograph had been in the follow-up subject data file. She had nearly lost her life in an incident six years before, but Suema herself had been unaware of that, so she was not even on the Towa Organization's checklist.

"No need to apologize," Suema gave her a gentle smile.

Aya was silent for a moment, then asked, "Um, Suema-sempai, can I ask you something?"

"What's that?"

"What do you think about Boogiepop?"

"Er…" Suema looked confused. "What do I think? Don't take this the wrong way, but that kind of rumor's a little…"

"You don't believe it?"

"Mmm…yeah, basically. But more than that, I just don't know anything about it."

"Really? But all of the girls…"

"Yep, all of them. Except me," Suema sighed. "They all think I'm morbid…like I know everything there is to know about murder. So nobody ever thinks to tell me about stuff like 'Boogiepop'…"

"Oh…"

"But you know, like, that sort of killer, or *shinigami* or whatever…it's so *blah*. Typical adolescent imagery. Everyone's anxious about something, so part of them feels like it would be just great if everything around them were destroyed. Like they want to be killed."

"———" Aya stiffened.

"And grown-ups are all irresponsibly saying crap like, 'This period of anxiety is only a phase. Things will get better soon.' Ha! Like that helps. Things just aren't that easy, right?" Suema's shoulders slumped. "That's where he comes in."

"Huh…?"

"Boogiepop. *That's why he exists.* To protect an unstable heart and…and keep it like that. That's all he is, I think. Course, you're probably happier believing in him," Suema added with a shrug, as if joking.

This unexpected answer confused Aya. "Protect?"

"Even though he's a *shinigami*? But that kind of thing's the product of romanticism, bred without much knowledge of actual assassins. Anyone who's actually killed someone would never put on some goofy ass costume. I mean, seriously!"

"…………" Aya lowered her gaze. Whatever Boogiepop was, he would not protect her, she thought. "Sempai, can I talk to you?" Her mouth moved before she thought. She had never before tried to talk to someone of her own accord like this.

"Sure," Suema nodded.

So readily that Aya's little mouth opened, "A boy…likes me. I think."

"Mm."

"But I…I'm no good. I can't do something…like that."

"Mm."

"I'm no good for him…but I don't know what to do."

"Mm."

"I'd do anything for him…but there's just nothing I can do.

And instead, I'm just causing all sorts of problems for him. What can I do…?" As she talked, she found herself shaking again. Her hands clutched her own shoulders, but that couldn't stop it.

"Mm," Suema nodded.

"I can't be hated by anybody. That's the way I am, but if this goes on, he's going to hate me…"

"Mm."

"But the only thing justifying my existence is that nobody hates me. But there's nothing I can do…nothing left for me to do. I'd be better off if I wasn't alive…"

"Impossible," Suema spoke at last. "It's impossible to live without someone hating you," she declared.

"Eh…?" Aya looked up.

Suema stared at her, peering into her eyes. Not accusingly, though. No, it was like the gaze of a mother looking at a sleeping child. Yet Orihata Aya had never been looked at that way before, so she was quite flustered.

"Being alive means you have to come into contact with other people. No matter how hard you try, you will end up hurting some of those people. There's nothing we can do about it. That's just life," Suema explained calmly. Her direct—yet gentle and soft—gaze made Aya feel like she was naked.

"B-but…"

"I'd bet good money on you already having made yourself several enemies. And not just any enemies. I'm talking people who hate you so much that they want to kill you," Suema said, the soft-ness of her tone contrasting with the harshness of her words.

"............" Aya was floored. She could form no answer. Her mouth opened, but barely formed words. "Wh-what…do you…?"

"That's the way things are," Suema said, answering without really answering. Yet it sounded awfully convincing. She continued, "The very idea of living without being hated is detestable. You may not mean it that way, but trying to not be hated is like violating another's right to hate you. See what I mean? *You're* the one hurting *them*," she said, heatedly.

"..............." Aya simply stared back at her. Suema's gaze never wavered.

"Not to change the subject or anything, but have you ever heard of a writer named Kirima Seiichi?" Suema asked.

"Huh?" Aya snapped out of it.

Suema nodded, "Well, he's a novelist, though, uh, I still haven't gotten to actually reading any of his fiction stuff. Anyway, in one of his psychology books, he wrote: 'There certainly is *something* out there. Something that makes people believe that they have to know their place in life. This knowledge gets in between people, and rocks the very foundations of this world.'" Suema spouted this quote off smoothly from memory. She thought it was perfectly normal, but her ability to produce things like this at the drop of a hat was one reason other people were so creeped out by her. She remained pretty oblivious to that, though. "'…If there is anything that gives value to human life, it is the struggle with that "something." In the battle with the Imaginator that does your thinking for you—*VS Imaginator* is the starting line on which all humans must stand.' Which is pretty hard to grasp, I know, but the point is, humans are all bound by the chains of common sense far more than we realize, and this is what makes us suffer."

"Chains…?"

"Right. If we're bound by something, we've got to cut ourselves loose; that's what he's going on about." Suema spoke of this writer like most people do when using a friend as an example.

"…………"

"I'm sure you have something you have to do, something that you can't live without doing. I'm not gonna ask you what that is, but that boy who likes you…he doesn't want you to be tying yourself into knots like this. That much I'm sure of."

"Yes," Aya nodded, hooked on Suema's words.

Suema grinned. "This is gonna sound pretty pompous, but I really think you're missing the concept of that 'struggle.' And you really need to get that."

"Yes…" she replied. But how could she get it?

Aya just gritted her teeth. She knew this girl was right.

"You can die after you fight. For now, let's get down from here. You're a new student, right?"

"Yes, I am…"

"Oh, no! The orientations have already started! We'd better hurry!"

***

I grabbed her hand and led her down from the roof.

When we reached the ground, she turned to me and bowed.

"Thank you. I don't know if I can do anything, but I'm going to try," she said.

I was a little flustered. I'm not really the best person to be dispensing life counseling. I'm more of the type to receive it. Yet it seemed like something I said must've sunken in.

"Yeah…sorry for rambling on like that," I said, honestly.

She shook her head. "No…um, sempai…?"

"Yes?"

"If the one I have to fight is Boogiepop, then should I still fight?" she asked, deadly serious.

Naturally, I replied, "Absolutely." I knew nothing about her, but I was making sweeping declarations.

"Thank you," she said again, and turned and ran.

Suddenly I realized something, and called after her, "What's your name?"

"Orihata Aya," she said, stopping, and bowing once more.

"Good luck, Orihata-san," I waved.

And for some reason, I had the strangest feeling that I would meet her again. I don't know how I knew this, but the sharp pain in my chest said I would.

VS Imaginator Part I – "SIGNS" closed.
To be continued in Part II "PARADE"

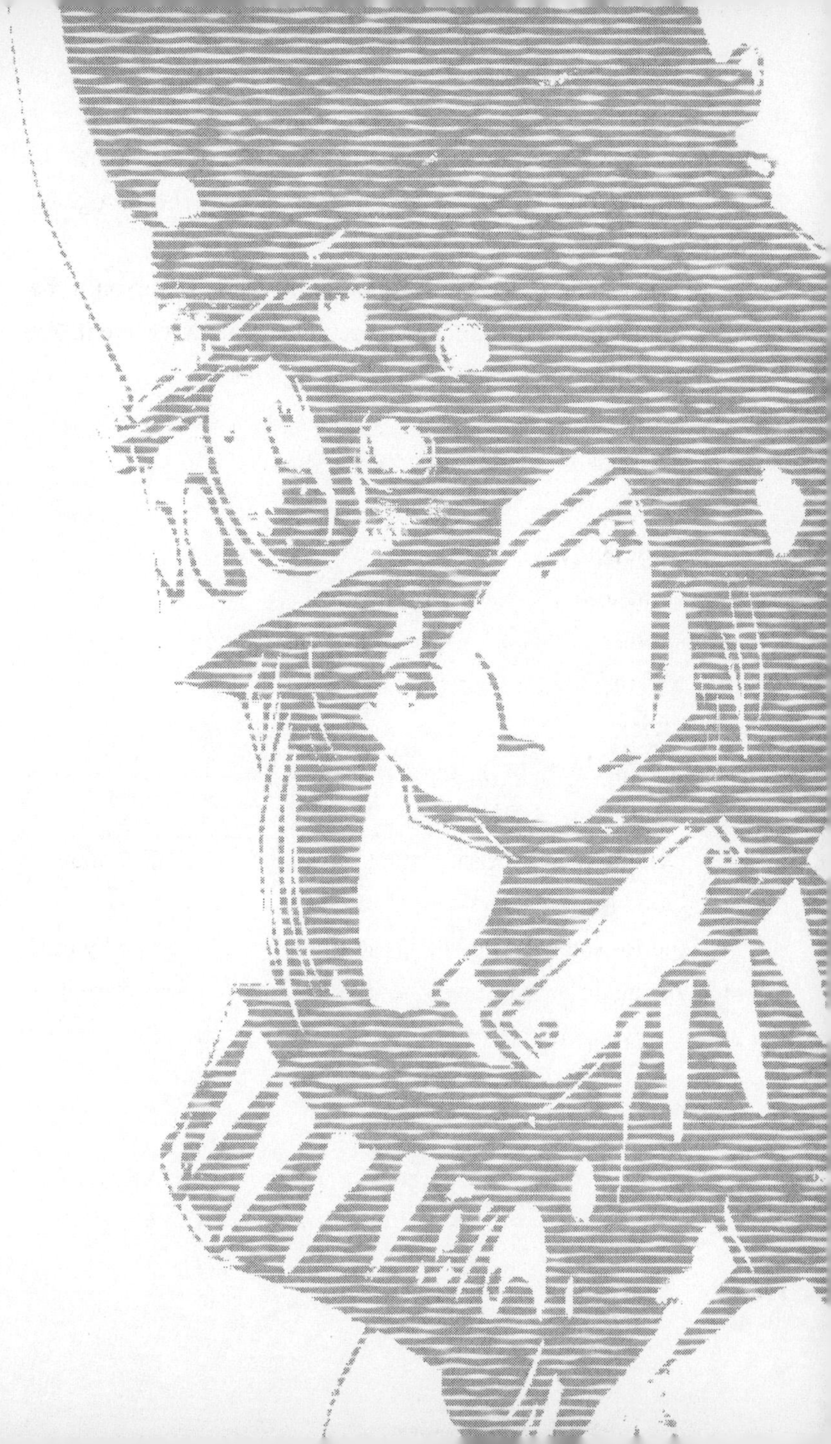

Afterword
That Thing with the Pop and the Boogie

There's something called pop culture. It's made up of novels, and manga, and movies, and games, and music, and just about anything else, really. Art? Nah, that's a little, you know, too artsy. Frankly, pop culture is a bit better at rocking people emotionally than the better chunk of the so-called fine arts. The sole standard of judgment in pop culture is the ludicrously simple concept of "what sells wins," which is nice and honest. Sells is sort of an "*enh*" term to me, so let's say that it finds an audience. It's a very pop culture thing to establish yourself by finding an audience. Which is true, and I tell people this, but I bet they'd say everything works that way, but in our world, there *are* things that are just so damn good no matter what other people say. And that sort of thing is not called pop culture. No, that's known as a lost masterpiece, or a legendary performance, or by all sorts of other names. It's not that these things aren't great—they just aren't pop.

I'm saying this in full knowledge that it might be misunderstood, but most pop culture is kind of half-assed. "The real thing is stuff, so fake stuff is better." Is that logical? People fully capable of making something real are deliberately pulling back and putting out something fake. What does this tell us? Thinking about that scares me, so I'm not going to, but this very half-assed approach is also sort of "blowing away the petrified past and opening a path to the future." (Nobody's got any idea of what I'm talking about, right?) (Okay.)

The best thing about pop culture is how hard it is to achieve any kind of legitimacy. It's not that it never earns it, but it's pretty rare. Something that was king of the hill a moment before is cast onto the compost heap a second later, while something that was long ago pronounced dated is resurrected and declared, "Innovative!" "Why did those idiots forget about this?" That's what pop is. It's pretty crazy, but within that whirlpool you do get a sense of a certain kind of necessity. Something appears, becomes huge, and then explodes, and is gone completely. Like a bubble…with a pop. Hmm, a fitting name. There's no cheap trick to get something established. A novel might win some big award, but that doesn't have the least bit of effect on sales.

To be perfectly honest, my own tastes have always been a bit disconnected from my generation. I'm the least pop person ever. I'm running around listening to stuff from twenty years ago, thirty years ago, screaming, "Awesome!", reading books from fifty years ago and shouting, "Coool!" Yes, that kind of guy. These things aren't connecting to the pop of today at all;

the only one getting excited is me. I'm a little worried about that. As someone who's trying somehow to make a living as a novelist, naturally I'm worried, and I'm trying to make myself more pop, but it just isn't working. As I can imagine that you can tell from the general tone of this essay, I admire pop and I have a sort of complex about it, really. But since my personality's gone and twisted itself, with everything I make people say, "Well…it's unique," or "Is this supposed to be funny?" And they usually follow it up with, "Well, *we* can't publish it…" They're still saying it, even now.

But even so, I've got to aim for pop. This is the theme of my life, so it can't be helped. If everything I make ends up being more boogie, it's not my fault…I'd like to say that, except it is my fault, really. But I'm going for it anyway. Even if it's a kind of boogie pop, then someday, I still might make the real thing.

(This guy just writes whatever crap he wants to…)
(Whatever.)

BGM "CHILDREN of the SUN" by MAYTE

CHARACTER ROLL CALL
by chapter

(F) = female   (M) = male   (O) = other

V

Anou Kumiko (F)
Anou Shinjirou (M)
Asukai Jin (M)
Miyashita Touka/Boogiepop (F)
Orihata Aya/Camille (F)
Spooky E (M)
Taniguchi Masaki (M)

VI

Anou Shinjirou (M)
Anou's Girlfriend (F)
Kinukawa Kotoe (F)
Miyashita Touka/Boogiepop (F)
Niitoki Kei (F)
Orihata Aya/Camille (F)
Suema Kazuko (F)

FRIENDS & COUPLES

Minahoshi Suiko (F)
Komiya Mariko (F)

Orihata Aya/Camille (F)
Taniguchi Masaki (M)

Asukai Jin (M)
Kinukawa Kotoe (F)

Kinukawa Kotoe (F)
Kinoshita Kyoko (F)

Miyashita Touka (F)
Suema Kazuko (F)

Yuriko (F)
Misaki (F)

THE "IN" CROWD
Movers and Shakers in the Boogiepop Universe

Asukai Jin (M)
Minahoshi Suiko/Imaginator (F)
Miyashita Touka (F) / Boogiepop (O)
Orihata Aya/Camille (F)
Spooky E (M)
Taniguchi Masaki/Boogiepop (M)

TIMELINE

	BOOGIEPOP and Others	BOOGIEPOP Returns VS Imaginator Part 1
HIGH SCHOOL 1st YEAR		■ Minahoshi Suiko's suicide.
HIGH SCHOOL 2nd YEAR	■ Kamikishiro Naoko asks Tanaka Shiro out. ■ The Manticore escapes from the Towa Organization's laboratory. ■ Saotome Masami meets the Manticore and begins killing students. ■ Takeda Keiji sees Boogiepop in town. ■ Kamikishiro meets Echoes. ■ Kirima Naki begins seriously investigating. ■ Boogiepop faces off against the Manticore. ■ The pillar of light pierces the sky.	■ Asukai Jin meets the Imaginator. ■ Taniguchi Masaki meets and falls in love with Orihata Aya. ■ Boogiepop fights Spooky E. ■ Taniguchi Masaki encounters Spooky E, begins dressing as Boogiepop.
HIGH SCHOOL 3rd YEAR		
RONIN YEARS	■ Kimura Akio receives a letter from an unidentified sender.	

TRANSLATION NOTES

Translating a foreign language work is a challenging task that can result in a lot of sleepless nights and headaches for the production team involved. The general rule of thumb for any English-language release is to make sure that it retains the intricacies of the source material, while not reading like a literal translation. It's a difficult line to walk, but we at Seven Seas believe that preserving cultural nuance is of utmost importance.

For this reason, we've strived to present a translation that is as close to the original as possible, while keeping the flow of the novel intact. The following pages of translation notes are presented here as a way to offer some additional insight into many of the terms, characters and other cultural items that you may not have understood while reading the novel. These notes also offer a further look into some of the choices that the editorial staff at Seven Seas had to make while bringing the work to you. Enjoy!

Cover

Imaginator vs Imaginater

For those familiar with the Japanese novels, you may have noticed that the books contradict themselves with regard to how to spell the word "Imaginator." In Japanese, "Imaginator" is consistently written one way, but in English it appears as both Imaginator" and "Imaginater."

"Imaginator" is the version that we will be using consistently throughout our *Boogiepop* translations as it seems to be the more accepted spelling, and frankly, is the one that sounds the coolest.

How does it appear in the Japanese book? Well, the spelling "Imaginater" can be found in English on the Japanese covers of novel 2 and 3 and within the color pages. However, this is contradicted by the interior text itself, which uses "Imaginator" in several places including the title page before Chapter I, and at the very end of Chapter VI, leading us to believe that this is Kadono-sensei's preferred spelling.

Prelude

Ifukube Akira (May 31, 1914-2006)

Ifukube-sensei is regarded by many as Toho's greatest and most beloved composer. While he is most famous for his contributions to the *Godzilla* series of films, Ifukube's body of work spans decades. **(pg. 21)**

Chapter 1

Signs vs Sign

The original Japanese edition of this second novel carries an interior subtitle in English, which dubs this book "Sign." In Japanese language, there is rarely any distinction between the singular and plural, so you usually have to figure out the singular or plural based on the context. Judging by the various foreshadowed events of this novel, we felt that it was appropriate to think of the signs as more than just one, which is why we retitled it as "Signs."

Saint-Exupery's *The Little Prince*

Known as *Le Petit Prince* in France, the 1943 novel is the most famous book by French aviator Antoine de Saint-Exupéry. The novel is a profound children's book that carries many idealistic points about life and love. In the book, the author imagines himself stranded in the Sahara Desert and meets a young extraterrestrial prince and the two have many deep conversations. The essence of the book is contained in the famous line uttered by the fox to the little prince: "On ne voit bien qu'avec le coeur, l'essentiel est invisible pour les yeux" (One sees rightly only with the heart, the essential is invisible to the eyes)." **(pg. 38)**

Chapter 11

Japanese ATMs

You might have noticed that Masaki tried to get money from an ATM, but it was off. In Japan, ATMs in Japan tend to close at 9 PM on weekdays. So next time you're in Japan, remember to hit the ATM before they close. **(pg. 77)**

Code Name Camille

The meaning of Aya's code name, Camille (literally pronounced as *Kamiiru* in Japanese), is anyone's guess; though, the 1936 movie *Camille* staring Greta Garbo (based on the 1852 novel *La Dame aux Camélias* by Alexandre Dumas, fils.) seems to relate to Aya thematically. The movie *Camille* tells the story of a light-hearted romance in 1840s Paris where a young woman wins the heart of a wealthy young man, but ultimately gives him up for his own good. The story itself later inspired such movies as *Pretty Woman* and *Moulin Rouge!* For continuity buffs, *Boogiepop* novel 13 entitled *Lost Mobius: Boogiepop Bounding* features Aya quite prominently. **(pg. 87)**

Chapter III

Shogi

A board game similar to chess in which two players go head-to-head with 20 wedge-shaped pieces each with the objective to checkmate their opponent's king. **(pg. 99)**

"I stared after her like I'd seen a fox."

Foxes, known as "kitsune" in Japanese, have traditionally appeared in Japanese folklore and mythology as deceivers and tricksters. According to legend, these animals possess great intelligence and a multitude of magical powers—including the ability to possess humans and to create illusions. In some tales, the kitsune have actually been known to take the shape of beautiful woman, pretty young girls or old men. **(pg. 102)**

Chapter V

Nori Bento

Every fan of Japanese anime should know that "bento" is a Japanese lunch box. "Nori" is seaweed. So, a *nori bento* consists of rice and seaweed only. **(pg. 145)**

Two Hundred Thousand Yen

Basically, this is a little less than $2000US dollars (at the current exchange rate, at least.) **(pg. 151)**

Yakisoba Shops

A Japanese restaurant that specializes in fried noodles. **(pg. 164)**

Join us now for a special sneak preview of
the third novel in the Boogiepop series.

Boogiepop
returns
VS Imaginator Part 2

written by
Kouhei Kadono

illustrated by
Kouji Ogata

english translation by
**Andrew
Cunningham**

Coming in
October 2006 from

Seven Seas

"Ow! Damn, cut myself!" Kinukawa Kotoe sucked the tip of her finger, scratched by one of the barbs on the fence around the abandoned amusement park. The taste of blood filled her mouth. "What am I *doing*?"

She reached into her school bag and took out one of the cartoon rabbit decorated band-aids that she always had with her, and wrapped it around her wound.

She felt very childish. Like she was three years old again.

Nobody knew she had a key to the half-finished Paisley Park construction site. One of the countless companies with a claim on the ground belonged to her father, and when he brought the master key home, Kotoe had snuck out of the house with it, and made a copy.

Ever since, it had become her secret hideout when she was feeling depressed.

The buildings in the park had been abandoned just after construction began, so they looked more like abstract sculptures than anything else, and the curved walking paths were all bare, waiting patiently for beautiful tiles to be laid upon them. But as Kotoe looked at the buildings as she walked, she felt as if she was about to cry a river.

It was a very lonely place, and while she might have been a cheerful girl at home and at school, something about the desolate, deserted park tugged at her heartstrings. She had never told anyone about it, but...

Part of her was convinced that she belonged in a place like this.

Like there was something fundamentally missing inside of her—a draft blowing through the cracks in her heart.

This place, where they had tried to build a spectacular amusement park, was now a forgotten, pathetic little dream—the kind of dream everyone has when they are young, but never achieves, only to become abandoned with time. Kotoe felt like she had never had that sort of dream at all.

Of course, this seventeen-year-old girl was not consciously aware of this. But she indistinctly felt it, and this sadness remained inside of her, refusing to melt away.

She walked on through the ruins, painted by the light of the setting sun.

As she did, she thought about the only thing she ever thought about these days—her cousin, Asukai Jin.

(Jin-niisan...)

She first met Asukai Jin when she was five years old, and she remembered it clearly, even now.

Jin's father had come to borrow money from his younger brother, Kotoe's father, and Jin had come along with him. He must still have been in elementary school.

She had only seen him from a distance.

Kotoe's father had taken his wife's name, Kinukawa, and he behaved like the rightful heir, much more so than Kotoe's docile mother. He had thundered, "Do not beg," at his brother.

But Jin's father had persisted, until Jin said, quietly, "Uncle Kouji's right, Father. Nobody would lend money to someone who just wants it without a plan for how to use it."

When that clean boy soprano cut through the tension in the drawing room (decorated perfectly to her father's tastes), Kotoe had the strangest feeling that this boy would take her away from everything—away from this life where she lacked nothing but could scarcely breathe.

Much to her father's surprise, his brother agreed with his son Jin, and abandoned his attempts to beg for money based solely upon familial blood ties, and instead began to explain the details of his business plan.

Kotoe didn't really understand the conversation from that point on, but ultimately, Kotoe's father did end up lending his brother some money. What Kotoe remembered was how Jin's farewell showed far better manners than his father's.

He seemed so noble.

He was her first love.

She had looked forward to seeing him again, but it turned out that the start-up business that Jin's father had founded with the borrowed money had gone bust. They didn't return to Kotoe's house for a very long time. Occasionally, her father would refer to his brother as "that good-for-nothing," which always made Kotoe extremely sad.

It was four years before Kotoe met Jin again.

Father and son called at the Kinukawa home once more. The father was extremely well-dressed, and, surprisingly, he returned the money that he had borrowed. Plus interest.

Kotoe's father muttered, "Normally, you would also have to pay damages..." but he was clearly happy to have the money back.

"But how did you get it?" he asked, but Jin's father just grinned.

His son sat next to him, in the uniform from his junior high school. He didn't appear bored by the grown ups' conversation, but he also did not appear to be excessively interested either.

He blended in so easily, and Kotoe, who was watching from the shadows, was mystified by this.

"Say, Kouji, would you like a painting?"

"Painting?"

"First rate artists only. I'm in that line of work now."

"*You* sell paintings? You got a D in art! How do you know you aren't selling fakes?"

"I leave all that up to him," he said, pointing at his son. "He's a genius. He's won all sorts of awards for his paintings."

"Really? But even so..."

"His eye is amazing. We buy stuff up at paltry sums, and a year later that artist explodes, and we sell it for ten times the price," he said proudly.

Even when praised, the boy stayed quiet.

"Oh? So someday you might become a great artist like Picasso, Jin?" Kotoe's father asked, addressing his nephew for the first time.

"That's my dream, sir," the boy replied, without a trace of arrogance. His manner proved that was the most together person in the room, Kotoe thought.

He knew what everyone in the room was thinking, and matched it. He was perfectly at ease, yet he never gave off even a hint of being such.

The evening developed into a drinking party, and Jin and his father spent the night at Kotoe's house.

Kotoe wanted desperately to talk with Jin, but he never left his father's side, and she never had the chance.

Only once, when Jin came to the kitchen to get a glass of water for his father's stomach pills, was she able to say, "Um…"

There she was, standing in front of him, the moment she'd been longing for.

"Oh, sorry. Can I get some water?" he asked politely.

"C-certainly!" Kotoe replied.

Her mother said, "What a good boy," and handed him a cup of water.

He bowed his head, and left.

Kotoe wanted to call after him, but she couldn't think of anything to say, and so she could only watch him leave.

But that evening, when Kotoe woke in the middle of the night and came down to the kitchen for a drink, she found Jin standing alone in the garden, looking up at the night sky.

It was winter outside, and all he had on were the pajamas they'd found for him, so it must have been terribly cold out.

He looked so sad. She'd never seem him look anything but calm, so Kotoe was a little shocked.

She wanted to know what he was thinking about, but she thought it must be something difficult that she wouldn't be able to understand. This meant she didn't know what to do. So she stood there for a while, and eventually he turned and spotted her.

"Ah…!" she exclaimed, and he bowed his head, and came over to the outside of the house.

Kotoe hurriedly unlocked the window. "Wh-what are you doing?" she asked. When she opened her mouth, a white cloud came out.

"Sorry, didn't mean to surprise you. I was just wondering if it would snow."

"Snow?"

"Yeah. It looked like it might, but…"

"You like snow?"

"Yeah. Childish of me, huh?" he grinned.

"Aren't you cold?" she asked, and instantly regretted it. What a stupid question.

But he didn't seem to notice. "Sure, it's cold. I was just about to come inside," he said softly, bobbed his head, and walked away.

Kotoe watched him go again.

At the time, they were just relatives. They had no other connection. So once again, quite some time passed without the two of them seeing each other.

(But…)

Kotoe stopped in front of the most eye-catching remnant, a spiral tower that was to have been named "The Ladder." Like Asukai Jin had done as a boy, she looked up at the sky.

But of course, it was not snowing. After all, it was April.

(But…Jin-niisan's father, so awful…)

His cause of death was still unclear.

He was walking along the street, and suddenly, he vomited up blood and fell over. It was all so sudden that the police suspected he'd been poisoned.

But there were no traces of anything like that. Witnesses had said that just before his death, he'd eaten lunch at a perfectly ordinary family restaurant. Nobody who worked at the restaurant had any connections to him. Clearly, it wasn't poison.

Even so, the whole ordeal left Asukai Jin orphaned.

"We should help him," Kotoe said.

Her mother asked, "Why don't we adopt him?"

But since her father had married into the family, he felt it would never do for him to take in his brother's child. Besides, Asukai Jin himself refused to entertain such notions, telling them not to worry.

His father's business was handed off to others, and most of the inheritance went to various debts and obligations, but Jin quickly secured a full scholarship to an art school, and a job as a cram school teacher took care of his living expenses. Very efficient.

Kotoe was somewhat relieved.

If they had adopted him, then she would have become his sister. Sure, it was a dream, but as long as they were cousins, the possibility remained.

But no matter how quickly Asukai Jin had taken charge of his situation, that sad boy who stared up at the night sky remained. Kotoe could still see it in him.

He had some sort of burden. He'd carried it for a very long time.

(And yet...)

Recently, Jin was acting strangely.

Wandering around all night long, coming back with what looked like bloodstains on his clothes...and even worse, he was oddly cheerful.

He had always been affable, easy to get along with and well liked. That hadn't changed, but...

The only person who had listened to her problems was a girl from her school named Suema Kazuko. They weren't close enough to be called friends, but she had listened carefully, and told her, "Why don't you leave things up to me?"

She had telephoned later and added, "I'll clear things up, but until then, you'd better stay away from him." Which meant Kotoe hadn't seen Jin for a while.

Suema Kazuko seemed reliable, and she would probably be able to figure things out far better than Kotoe herself could ever manage. But she still missed him.

"Jin-niisan..." she whispered, looking up at the red sky.

"Is that your man's name?" a voice asked from behind her.

Surprised, she tried to turn around, but the electric monster's hands had already latched onto each side of her head.

There was a crackle, and she could feel her brain's functions rudely interrupted.

"............?!"

Kinukawa Kotoe was unconscious.

***

"Her name's Kinukawa Kotoe, and she's seventeen, eh?" Spooky E had gone through the pockets of his newly acquired prey, and found her Shinyo Academy student ID.

"So, that's how she had a master key," the monster whispered, glancing over towards a sign at the side of the park. The name "Kinukawa Enterprises" was printed on it.

"Damn, she's loaded..."

Had she been awake, she would have shuddered at the sight of the sinister smile that split Spooky E's face from ear to ear. His big round eyes stayed wide open, making it even more horrible.

"Which means she's got cash. Perfect. I can use her to find this 'Imaginator.'"

The monster licked his fingers, and thrusted his saliva-drenched hands into Kotoe's beautifully treated hair.

To be continued in

VS Imaginator Part 2

Coming in October 2006

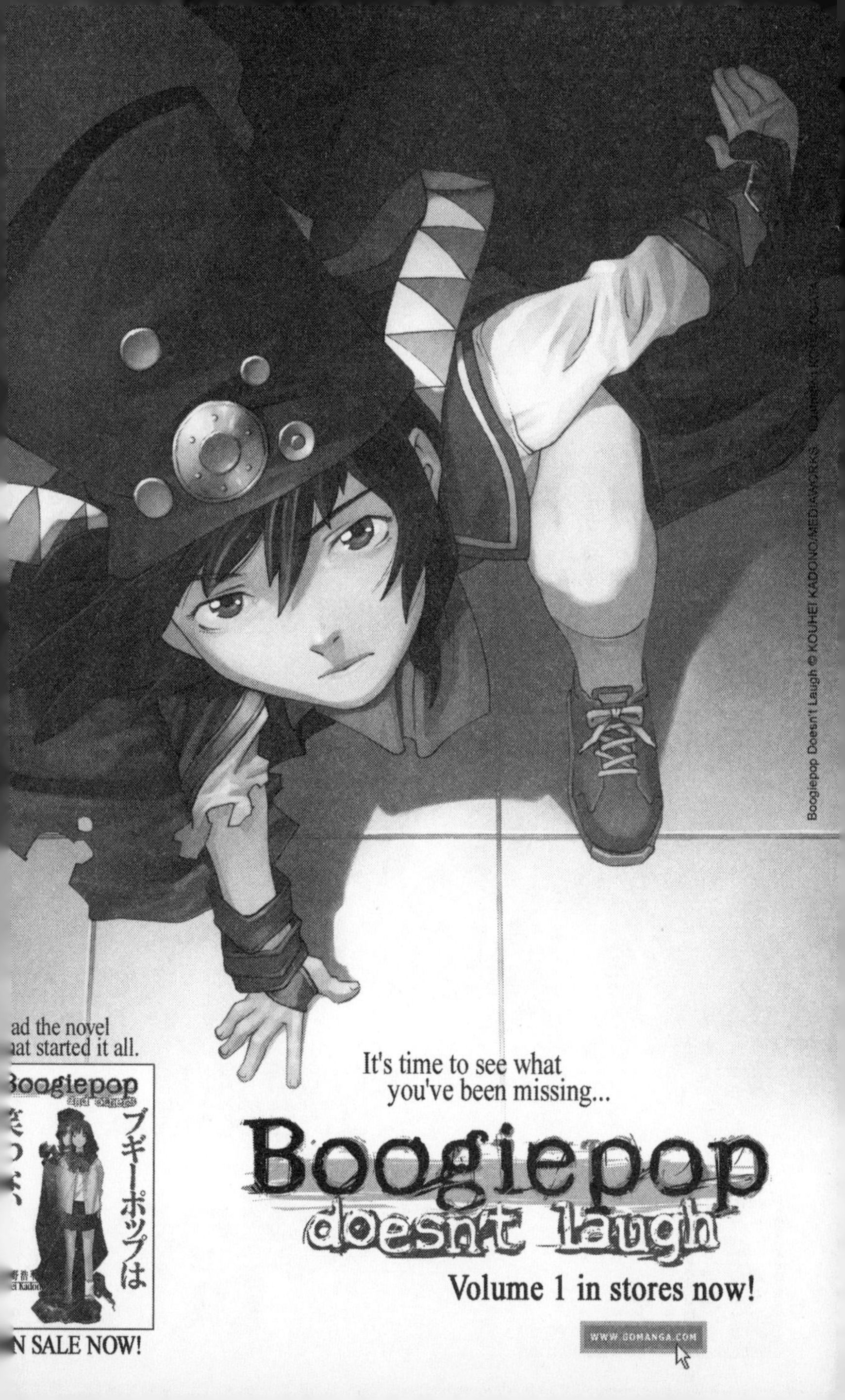

ad the novel
hat started it all.
Boogiepop
ブギーポップは
N SALE NOW!
It's time to see what
you've been missing...
Boogiepop
doesn't laugh
Volume 1 in stores now!
WWW.GOMANGA.COM
Boogiepop Doesn't Laugh © KOUHEI KADONO/MEDIAWORKS

The face of the night.

A relentless shadow.

Perhaps death itself.

ブギーポップは
Boogiepop 笑わない
Phantom

You've read the novel, now see the anime!